Hardwired to Learn

Leveraging the Self-Sustaining Power

Power

of Lifelong Learning

by Teri Hart

CHAKRA7 PRESS

Hardwired to Learn: Leveraging the Self-Sustaining Power of Lifelong Learning

Copyright © 2021 Teri Hart

All rights reserved. No part of this book may be reproduced or reprinted in any form or by any means, electronic or mechanical, including photocopying, recording, or by any information storage and retrieval system, without permission in writing from the publisher.

For information regarding permission to reprint material from this book, please email your request to: terihart@hardwiredtolearn.com

Please purchase only authorized electronic editions of this work and do not participate in or encourage piracy of copyrighted materials, electronically or otherwise. Your support of the author's rights is appreciated.

Printed in the United States of America
Chakra7 Press
An imprint of Chakra7, LLC

Cover design by: Darko Bovan
Book design by: Paula Schlauch

ISBN: 978-0-578-30007-8

The field of learning and development attracts the most curious, courageous, and empathetic people one could know. Collectively, my colleagues—bosses, peers, team members, as well as those working for learning vendors, think tanks, and learning exchanges—have encouraged me with their passion, humbled me with their expertise, and fueled me with their love for learning.

So, it is no surprise that as I look back at my journey in learning and development, I am most grateful for the many colleagues with whom I've had the opportunity to work. From them, I have learned so much, not only about the profession of learning but about myself. If the future depends, at least in part, on corporate learning and development organizations, it is in good hands.

It is to these amazing colleagues that I dedicate this book.

I also dedicate this to my two children, River and Sage, who inspired me to reach when I didn't know I could.

Contents

Introduction

"The beautiful thing about learning is nobody can take it away from you."

—B.B. King

Recently, I taught a learning and development session for aspiring leaders and shared the story of Howard Thurman, a renowned American educator, prominent theologian, and civil rights leader. Thurman was born on the eve of the 20th century. When he turned 14 in 1913, he had the opportunity to attend the Florida Baptist Academy in Jacksonville, Florida, one hundred miles from his home in Daytona Beach. At the time, the academy was one of only three high schools for African Americans in Florida, so this opportunity, though far from home, was potentially life-changing for the young teen.

At the train station in Daytona Beach, Thurman discovered that though he had enough money for train fare, he didn't have enough to check his trunk that held all his belongings. A stranger who noticed how distraught the boy was offered to cover the cost of his luggage. The young Thurman never forgot the act of kindness that instantly restored what would be a trajectory of lifelong learning and a heartfelt purpose to ignite others to pursue their passions.

Learning is transcendent. What other innate human capability improves with time and use? Learning makes us

1

more resilient to stress, can help us solve the world's biggest problems, and has the capacity to profoundly affect our own life as well as the lives of others.

Yet, we tend to take learning for granted. We undervalue it, underestimate its potential, and sometimes resist it altogether as we would resist a plate of our least-favorite vegetable. Some say they're *"done with learning,"* even though they cannot possibly stop the process, for even in our restorative dreams, we learn. I believe neuroscience will one day prove that we haven't even scratched the surface on human potential to learn.

This is good news because it has never been more important to be a learner. The double disruption of the 4th Industrial Revolution and the COVID-19 pandemic has created an unparalleled level of uncertainty about the future of work for people of every age, in every country, and in all walks of life. Add to that the threat of global climate change and ongoing threats to social equality that undermine the lives of those they marginalize and the long-term health of the communities in which we live. We have a lot to learn and much work to do if we are to be resilient and adapt to our changing world.

I discovered an appreciation for learning at a young age, inspired by the idea it was something personal I could do for myself, something that nobody could take away. Later, I came to view learning as "a way out." I learned my way out of the self-limiting beliefs that I developed in my formative years; I learned my way out of the struggles of job loss and small business ownership, and I learned my way out of the financial and emotional burden of single parenting.

Similarly, I also "learned in" throughout my life (no, not a typo but my terminology for "leaning in" to the discomfort of learning). Let's face it; unless someone invents the technology that enabled Keanu Reeves's character Neo in the film *The Matrix* to upload kung fu abilities directly into his cortex, learning is uncomfortable.

We *learn in* any time we explore our curiosity, with or without aim. We *learn in* when we pursue a college degree, develop a skill like playing tennis, or seek to understand another's perspective. We *learn in* when we learn for the sake of learning and find joy in the process of discovery.

I have one goal for this book: to impart a way of thinking that will allow more people to transcend their perceived limitations. Whether we're acquiring an education, improving our health, or learning a skill that can enhance our lives, learning is life-affirming. The opportunity for learning is all around us, and our ability to access and accumulate endless knowledge has accelerated through digital technology.

Some friends of mine recently left suburban life behind and bought several acres in the country with the intent of living a more self-sustaining life, running their own business, and partially living off the land. When I asked how they were going to tackle the challenges of running their business and caring for their property and newly acquired chickens, they explained that everything they needed to know is online, from planting and harvesting Christmas trees to raising chickens. You don't have to look far for opportunities to learn.

One thing I've discovered is that learning begets learning. Once you demonstrate to yourself that you can do something that you never thought possible, it builds your confidence to do something else, perhaps previously unimaginable. I saw an example of this recently while following #lifelonglearning on Instagram.

A home-schooling mom in the middle of a math lesson with her "tween" determined that she wanted to be a role model to her child and learn the math that she was trying to teach her daughter. Previously, overseeing math lessons was her engineer husband's responsibility. But during this particular lesson, the mom realized how critical it was for her to understand the math herself, and in doing so, discovered her own potential for learning math, something she never thought possible. She expressed her excitement and heightened confidence in herself in her Instagram post: *I can learn math!*

In addition to being a lifelong learner, I've had the good fortune of being able to pursue learning as a vocation. I spent the earlier part of my career writing and designing hundreds of training courses and leadership programs.

Over the last two decades, I've studied the psychology and neuroscience of how people learn and have absorbed knowledge from the best and brightest colleagues at the great companies where I've had the good fortune to work. I've discovered a great deal about how we learn and how some of us become lifelong learners throughout this time.

This exposure to learning has engendered in me a profound appreciation for what the practice of learning is capable of: strengthening our minds, making us resilient to change, and upgrading who we are. Those who sagely told me at different times in my life that people can't change have been wrong. You *can* change! We now know that the human brain is endlessly firing and forming new neural pathways and connections. There is hope for all of us, and that hope is as enduring as the human race.

We are hardwired to learn. The human brain's learning infrastructure is made up of roughly 86 *billion* neurons linked to one another through *hundreds of trillions* of connections called synapses that communicate and pass along information every waking and sleeping moment. The number of neurons and synapses occurring in the human brain is unparalleled in nature, equipping humanity with boundless cognitive abilities.

We humans have a limitless potential to learn, and as you'll discover from this book, we as a species are growing more intelligent as time passes. This news of ourselves, revealed only recently through brain-imaging technology, should encourage each and every one of us to trust in our ability to learn and develop new skills.

I hope that the knowledge you gain about yourself and your abilities from this book will encourage and help you to not only become a better learner, but also help you grab the reins of your own well-being. Through learning, you can expand on your life's work or excel in a new career. You can change and adapt and grow more resilient and confident as the world changes around you.

Hardwired to Learn is organized into five parts.

Part 1 sets the stage by highlighting the industrial revolutions of the past and the social changes and disruptions brought by each. I describe why this, the 4th Industrial Revolution (4IR), may be the most pervasive and disruptive, and I provide examples of how the double disruption of technology and the pandemic is altering the world of work. I contend that the only way we can become resilient, adapt, and thrive is by embracing—and accelerating—our extraordinary capability to learn.

Part 2 recaps the origins of our ideas about learning and how the evolution of those theories over the past several hundred years has deepened our knowledge of ourselves and how we learn. I then expose what I believe are the four most prevalent myths of learning that have constrained the capacity of generations of children and adults to learn and grow. You will learn of the most recent discoveries in neuroscience and how these new insights are significantly altering our understanding of how the brain learns—potentially opening the door for a paradigm shift in human learning.

Part 3 identifies what's getting in the way of our capacity to learn and sets the stage for overcoming these barriers. I'll reveal how these obstacles that we impose on ourselves and others are widespread in education and training today, discouraging children and adults alike from applying themselves fully and providing a justification for those not willing to try harder. I share concrete strategies for unleashing your potential to learn.

Part 4 offers some tangible steps to get you started on your learning practice, from setting an intention to learn, to managing your health and well-being, and to improving cognitive capability. In addition to providing the mindsets and methods you can use to become a lifelong learner, I share research on how you can slow down the brain's aging process. I also share some learning hacks that will create a framework for how to think about learning.

Part 5—the final chapter—brings this all together by providing historical examples of how and why a Human Intelligence (HI) revolution is needed to accelerate our abilities in the face of the challenges of our time. I highlight the recent progress we've made and explore how we can address our challenges and opportunities through learning.

This book is not a miracle cure. I don't know of any five-step process for becoming smarter or mastering a particular subject; I know no simple trick to multiplying your ability to memorize facts or learn a new language. The science on improving memory is controversial and not addressed here. Lifelong learning is a lifelong journey, and as such, this book is written to help you adopt learning as an intentional practice and welcomed partner in all aspects of your life.

When I think about investing time in learning, I often think of that poignant statement uttered by the character "Red" in the film *Shawshank Redemption,* as he reflects on the rest of his life once he's paroled…with a tiny change:

Get busy *learning,* or get busy dying.

Don't wait. While we never stop learning, our potential does begin to decelerate with age. The time is now. This is an invitation to discover your own capabilities and live into your own inexhaustible, undeniable potential to learn.

—Teri Hart

Part 1

The Convergence of Things

1
At a Crossroads

Learning is what most people will do for a living in the 21st century.

— Alfred Edward Perlman

Before desktop computing, the Internet, and smartphones, Alfred Perlman, a retired railroad executive responsible for modernizing much of the railroad system in the United States in the mid-1900s, noticed that data-processing machines and automatic machine tools were more often performing routine and laborious tasks.

Commenting in 1962 on the use of computerized networks on the Penn Central train system, particularly in the replacement of office clerical duties and rail yard operations, Perlman said:

> *"Let me describe briefly what we have already done toward cybernation in the railroad industry and what we hope to do in the future. Like many other industries, we are using data processing machines to replace routine, repetitive clerical work. In addition, we have automatic machine tools, which perform their work faster and more efficiently without human intervention. We have maintenance-of-way*

equipment, which performs many laborious, complicated and delicate operations automatically. We are, in short, like most of industry, automating simple control functions that require only low-level human judgment."

As early as 1962, Perlman was talking about digital technology replacing humans in the railroad industry, beginning with Penn Central. Later, but well before he died in 1983, Perlman predicted that in the future, everyone would need to be a learner. His remarkable insights were ahead of his time, likely influenced by being a learner himself (an alumnus of MIT and Harvard Business School) and having dedicated his career to continually improving railroads.[1]

Eliminated by a Digital Upgrade

The digital technology transformation has been underway for over half a century since the advent of computing. Digital technology is a broad term that can refer to anything that relies on computers, including websites, apps, artificial intelligence (AI), robotic process automation, Internet of Things (IoT), and big data. Digital transformation is the adaptation of digital technology into all areas of business and human life.

You may have noticed the line at the Starbuck's counter getting smaller. That's because, according to their 2020 fiscal report, nearly one in four purchases are being made on the coffeehouse giant's mobile app.[2] Similarly, self-checkout lanes in grocery and big box stores are now as ubiquitous as self-serve gas and ATMs. These kinds of changes slowly reduce the need for people, or as we are finding in some industries and job functions, eliminate the need for human workers altogether.

In the past, automation primarily affected workers on the lower end of the pay spectrum, such as blue-collar workers performing physical, high-routine labor. Increasingly, those at the higher end, even in the white-color service industry, are finding their jobs being automated as well.

Consider the role of tax preparers and accountants in the age of TurboTax®. While increasingly more taxpayers are leveraging online software to file their taxes at home, corporations are increasingly employing digital technology to automate their transactions, resolve variances, reduce risks, and deliver insights. There are over one million accountants in the U.S, many of whom are finding their jobs evolving as routine accounting tasks are handled by software programs.

Yet, despite the automation, we will still need accountants and financial analysts in the future. Technology may be displacing human work, but it is also freeing up individuals for more interesting, challenging work. While the field of accounting is witnessing the adoption of analytics, robotic process automation, and distributed ledger technology like Blockchain, this mechanization is *augmenting* human work, not replacing it. Increasingly, accountants will be relied upon to flag ethical dilemmas, problem-solve, and use advanced technologies to bring more value to their clients. But to stay relevant, accountants, financial analysts, and other white-collar service professionals will need to learn new skills.

In a more transformative sense, what we now define as the 4th Industrial Revolution (4IR) may turn out to be the most ubiquitous and disruptive revolution since industry began. Before we dive into how 4IR is bringing about unprecedented change, let's look at how each of our revolutions has guided the advancement of our species and placed us on the doorstep of where we stand today.

Standing at a Threshold

Beginning with the introduction of the steam engine at the turn the 18th century, the **1st Industrial Revolution** represented our initial shift from reliance on domesticated animals and human effort. For the first time, the production of goods was mechanized. The first application was in textiles, transferring the manufacture of fabrics and clothing from people's homes to factories. The textiles were distributed broadly via the transcontinental railroad, the Internet of the 18th century, connecting the United States through trade from coast to coast.

The first revolution didn't end there. The invention of the telegraph transformed communications and industries, most dramatically, banking. These developments drove a wave of social change as people increasingly left their cottage industries and farming communities to live and work in the cities as populations became industrialized and urbanized.[3]

Electricity and advances in the development of steel helped build factories and fuel mass production, the hallmarks of the **2nd Industrial Revolution**. For many, the shift from farming to factory work must have been physically exhausting and felt unnatural as workdays were no longer organized around seasons and sunlight. Yet, life became a lot easier and more relaxed for so many people. Americans became truly mobile for the first time as trains and automobiles made it far easier and comfortable to travel. News of events spread through newspapers in every city, and the invention of the radio brought news and entertainment immediately and directly to millions of homes.[4]

Beginning in the late 1900s, the **3rd Industrial Revolution**—the Digital Revolution—enabled the spread of automation and digitization through computers and other electronics. One of the early models, the ENIAC (Electronic Numerical Integrator And Computer), built between 1943 and 1945, was the first large-scale, programmable, digital computer to run at electronic speed without the need for human or mechanical intervention.[5]

In essence, the global economy was computerized by the end of the 20th century. The invention of computing brought semiconductors and mainframe computing in the 1950s, desktop computing in the 1980s, and the linking of desktops via the Internet in the 1990s. This all led to the increasing automation of manufacturing and the huge disruption of industries such as banking, energy, and communications.

The **4th Industrial Revolution**, what we're on the precipice of now, represents the use of emergent digital technologies for previously unimaginable capabilities, blurring the line between human and machine and extending human capabilities exponentially. This latest revolution has brought about a slew of advanced digital capabilities such as Internet of Things (IoT), machine learning, artificial intelligence (AI), and robotics. There have also been significant scientific advancements in three-dimensional printing, magnetic resonance imaging (MRI), and genome mapping and editing.

In the October 2020 *The Future of Jobs Report*, the World Economic Forum made some stunning projections on the future of work, including assessments about the nature of work humans will be engaged in. According to the report, by 2025:[6]

- Half of the workforce will need reskilling for new jobs due to emerging technologies replacing the work they're doing now.

- Those remaining in their roles will still need to upgrade as much as 40 percent of their skillset.

- For the first time, work will be equally divided between humans and machines, with digital applications and automation shouldering more of the repetitive tasks, enhancing human work, and freeing up human capacity for different and more interesting work.

- Roles that leverage human-specific skills will increase in demand.

We see this happening in our daily lives. Consider how we are increasingly finding ourselves interacting with "bots" or software programs. Take a "chatbot" for instance—a software application that mimics human dialog and enables somewhat conversational interaction between humans (customers) and machines (companies).

Chatbots routinely conduct transactions such as taking orders, checking inventory, making product recommendations, confirming shipments, and processing returns. More advanced bots can leverage machine learning and language processing to interact with humans and make decisions that a human operator would otherwise make.

These little computer programs are becoming commonplace in some workplace roles, especially in customer service. According to LivePerson's website, HSBC and Virgin Atlantic are using their Conversational AI tool to respond to customer inquiries coming into their call centers. Some experts predict that as much as 90 percent of customer interactions in financial services will be automated by 2022.[7]

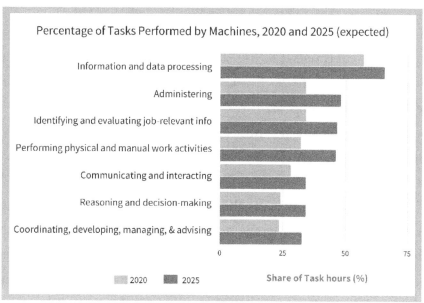

Humans vs. Machines: *The 2020 Future of Jobs Report highlights the types of tasks that will increasingly be performed by robots in the next five years.*[8]

These examples, and a multitude of others, describe how the nature of work will result in three potential job outcomes for people. If a chatbot performing simpler tasks replaces a human employee, the outcome is employee *displacement*. However, as in the case of HSBC, employees will be *reallocated* into newly-created roles, such as Conversation Designer and Chatbot Manager, to optimize the performance of chatbots.

Lastly, with chatbots performing simpler functions, employees such as financial analysts and accountants will experience *work augmentation*, freeing their time up for more complex and skills-developing tasks. One company that is initiating all three outcomes out of necessity and shaping the nature of work is Amazon.

The Fastest River in the World

It is said that in 1995, Jeff Bezos named his new company "Amazon" because it is the largest river in the world, and he wanted Amazon to be the largest bookstore in the world. In terms of length and size, however, the Nile has the Amazon beat by a little over 100 miles. More accurately, the Amazon is the fastest river in the world, five times faster than its next competitor for the top spot, the Congo.

Clearly, Amazon leads the robotics race in ecommerce and is already transforming the entire warehouse industry, which today employs more than 1.1 million Americans.[9] Amazon began automating its processes from the start and now has one of the most advanced fulfillment networks in the world. Autonomous mobile robots and aerial drones have both replaced and augmented human work in inventory-picking, sorting, packing, and shipping in thousands of warehouses around the globe.

The rise of robots and the pace of upgrades suggests that warehouse robots will soon be capable of effectively replacing every human task and, ultimately, every human warehouse employee. This also means that robots have the potential to eliminate some of the most menial of warehouse labor, freeing up people to perform more valuable and complex work. For example, Amazon robots now transport products across massive warehouses in place of workers who had to walk the equivalent of 10 or more miles a day.[10]

Amazon Scout: *In addition to robots in the warehouse, the company has developed Amazon Scout to deliver packages.[11]*

In 2019, Amazon announced plans to "upskill" 100,000 of its U.S. employees, including warehouse workers. The company cited a "changing jobs landscape" as the motivation for the job-training push. Employees in corporate offices and warehouses will have access to training programs to help them gain the necessary skills to move into higher-skilled, better paying, technical, and non-technical roles.[12]

Robots may be on the rise, but Amazon is hiring a lot of humans. In the first ten months of 2020, Amazon added 427,300 employees, bringing its global workforce to more than 1.2 million, up more than 50 percent from the prior year.[13] Amazon hired more software engineers and hardware specialists to address the increasing demand for cloud computing brought about by the explosive growth in streaming entertainment and electronic devices, which boomed during the pandemic.[14]

Amazon's rapid employee growth is unequaled in American history. The additional workers comprised twice the number of employees that Walmart added in a single year in 2002 when the company went global with its superstores. Before that, the closest comparisons are the kinds of hiring entire industries carried out in wartime, such as shipbuilding during the early years of World War II or home building immediately following the war.[15]

Accelerating Automation

By the summer of 2020, the pandemic had kept people out of nearly every kind of retail outlet. This created a watershed moment for ordering online and caused Amazon to grow at a spectacular rate. The company found itself fulfilling more orders than ever, and Federal Express, United Parcel Service, and a slew of smaller delivery services delivered more packages than ever before.

While Amazon's online sales soared along with coronavirus fears, the pandemic brought about a sort of "digital new world order" where technology adoption curves were shortened. In retail, we saw a shift from fragmented, multi-channel retailers to a single huge player that is extraordinarily efficient and whose technological developments are creating a tsunami of opportunity for growth and efficiency in other sectors.

As an example, in January 2021, General Motors unveiled their new startup, BrightDrop, their marque electronic delivery vehicle, and declared their intent to create "an ecosystem of electric products" to be used as "last mile" delivery options for online customers. Initial trials through a pilot program with Federal Express showed that these vehicles could deliver 25 percent more packages a day than a delivery driver alone.[16] In February 2021, fleet operator Merchants Fleet announced plans to procure 12,600 BrightDrop EV600 vehicles.[17]

In another example, Brain Corp, an AI company creating core technology in the robotics industry, surpassed two million hours of global operation, powering the world's largest fleet of autonomous commercial mobile robots. Robotic usage among U.S. retailers rose by 13.8 percent during the first quarter of 2020, compared to the same period the previous year, and jumped by 24 percent during the second quarter of 2020.[18]

Double Disruption

Very few companies have the resources of Amazon. And though the company may be upskilling some of its workers to prepare them for a new world of work, you might wonder who is reskilling the workers previously employed by Macy's, Lord & Taylor, Nordstrom's, JC Penney, and others. Unless they're now working at Amazon, Target, or Walmart (two other retailers stepping up their use of automation for online sales), some of these workers have been quietly displaced by mobile shopping apps and warehouse bots.

This retail apocalypse has been going on for years due to the gradual widespread adoption of online shopping and the acceleration of that trend through mobile apps that allow people to shop from any place at any time. But the pandemic accelerated that adoption, which had a catastrophic effect on brick-and-mortar retail and made Amazon larger than the nine next largest American retailers combined.[19] This devastating blow resulted in a sort of double disruption, which landed like a one-two punch on the retail sector.

Some companies were quicker to adapt. Target saw a 20 percent increase in comparable sales from 2019 to 2020, gaining $9 billion in total market share and growing revenue by $15 billion, more than in the 11 previous years combined. Online sales more than doubled, aided by Target's drive-up and pick-up options, while comparable sales in its brick-and-mortar stores grew 6.9 percent.[20] Due to its truly global footprint and high demand for its staple products during the pandemic, Walmart did not budge from its worldwide top revenue spot, surpassing Amazon's total 2020 revenue of $386 billion by $173 billion.[21]

The double disruption affected more than just the retail sector. The pandemic has accelerated a variety of technological tipping points. For example, during the crisis, more employees than ever were working from home. Online collaboration tools such as Microsoft Teams, WebEx, and Zoom were in huge demand. And Adobe's portable document format finally found its saturation point as digital signatures, and mail scanning became the norm. Telehealth gained traction, and more companies digitized online purchasing and customer interactions to meet increased demand for online transactions.

In addition to the direct impacts of people working from home, the pandemic illuminated new risks and the need for businesses to maintain strategic relevance, spurring unprecedented investment in digitization. McKinsey, a worldwide management consulting firm, revealed survey results suggesting that the pandemic sped up the adoption of digital technology by several years.[22]

Although the disruption to the retail sector has resulted in a combination of displacements, reallocations, and augmentations, there is likely to be much more displacement. Economists at the University of Chicago estimated that 32 to 42 percent of the job losses due to the pandemic will be permanent.[23] In its report, *The future of work after COVID-19*, the McKinsey Global Institute estimated that 25 percent of workers will need to reskill for new jobs.[24]

Humans Wanted

Perhaps as you're reading this, you think the situation is quite dire for us humans. After all, the shift from people doing most of the work to technology doing most of the work will undoubtedly surface new challenges and questions, whose solutions may very well decide the fates of our families and communities, and perhaps human society as a whole. We know we will have to navigate situations in the very near future that are currently unknown to us.

Klaus Schwab, Founder and Executive Chairman of the World Economic Forum and author of, *The Fourth Industrial Revolution*, states that much like the revolutions that preceded it, *"The Fourth Industrial Revolution has the potential to raise global income levels and improve the quality of life for populations around the world."* To be balanced in his assessment, Schwab also suggests that it could lead to greater inequality, *"...particularly in its potential to disrupt labor markets."*[25]

Through the lens of history, we know that industrial revolutions bring both good and bad. It is the paradox of progress that enabling a better, more affluent world presents both danger and disadvantage for many. Given that understanding, we have a unique opportunity to be deliberate in how we shape our future.

To create the best outcome, we must bring our best selves to the forefront. That means being both agile and resilient in the face of change. It requires us lifting all those around us to live into our shared but uniquely human capability. Bringing our best selves inherently requires human thinking and reasoning, which places *learning* squarely at the center of the opportunity and the *only* tool at our disposal.

Human Intelligence (HI) is more important than ever. Humans will be needed to focus on managing, advising, decision-making, reasoning, communicating, and interacting with an increasingly mechanized world. More emphasis will be placed on organizations and individuals to acquire skills such as critical thinking, problem-solving, and collaboration. Focus will be placed on a greater need for self-management in areas such as learning agility, resilience, stress tolerance, and flexibility.

You do not need to look far to find examples of what can happen when we employ Artificial Intelligence (AI) without Human Intelligence (HI). Consider the embarrassment Apple faced in 2019 when the algorithm responsible for credit limit decisions was implicated in possible gender bias.[26] While regulators did not find evidence of disparate impact caused by the algorithms, the public relations snafu highlighted the dangers of relying on technology without the critical view of HI.

Humans have the potential to be more forward-thinking and leverage human-only skills to improve the outcomes of AI. For example, banking analytics engines require HI to make sure they aren't inadvertently red lining—a discriminatory practice by lenders to deny loans, insurance, and other financial services to certain people or particular areas of a city or township. Also, technology-based health treatment such as gene-editing calls into question a number of ethical dilemmas that require assistance only humans can provide.

When you think about it, given the power we are now placing in the hands of technology, skilled people are needed more than ever to monitor, verify, and enhance the performance of that technology through creative and critical thinking as well as ethical decision-making.

A Paradigm Shift in Learning

Throughout the history of humankind, we have adapted to change and challenges through a process of learning and unlearning. Understanding and growth often emerge from grave or difficult situations, and our brains have responded to these kinds of stresses by continually adapting, growing, and evolving.

Before the pandemic, the central theme of discussions in corporate learning centered on the "skills gap," and data on the extent of that gap was abundant. PwC's survey of CEOs in 2019 found that "availability of skills" ranked third in the top ten threats to organizational sustainability. Of those CEOs polled, 80 percent said their people's lack of skills was a serious threat to their company's growth.[27]

Other surveys echoed the same sentiment, raising concern among corporate leaders. Were they doing all they could to attract the best talent and hire as many engineers, computer scientists, and big data scientists as possible in the face of a potential shortage of skilled human resources?

The double disruption has resulted in shortages of some talent and surpluses of others. There is only one way to balance the supply and demand of talent, and that is through learning. We must take up learning as a lifelong practice if we are to usher in the best possible conclusion to 4IR and inform us how to address the greater complexities of the next industrial revolution.

Everyone can learn. Moreover, as you will read in the chapters that follow, the potential of Human Intelligence (HI) is equally as amazing and perhaps even more remarkable than the potential of Artificial Intelligence (AI). Consider the roughly 86 billion neurons linked to one another through hundreds of trillions of synapses in our 3-pound brain.[28] Lighter than most laptops and powered by one-sixth the power of a 60-watt lightbulb, our brains are capable of limitless growth and change.

Beyond maximizing our innate capacity to learn, neuroscience is shedding light on learning mechanisms, creating more understanding around how humans learn—so much so that what we will know will inevitably usher in a paradigm shift of learning and unleash new potential for HI.

We face some enormous challenges as we prepare for the future. In addition to the task of adapting our skills to the evolving landscape of work, we face ethical and moral dilemmas around technology adoption, climate change, and deepening inequalities of opportunity in our society. This double disruption has far-reaching implications.

Working through these challenges will require critical thinking, collaboration, and empathy. In addition, for our own survival—and happiness—each of us needs to be both willing to learn and adept at learning. There is no other tool we can use that gives us the innate capability to be so resilient and adaptable to change—hope for prevailing as a species in the face of the mounting challenges and limitless opportunities to learn.

There is a good chance that the career you're working hard at building and advancing now may require a different set of skills in the future. Or perhaps you will be engaged in something unlike anything you're involved in currently. In any event, your ability to thrive will depend on your becoming more agile, more resilient, and open to learning, not just this month or this year, but throughout your life.

Alfred Perlman, the railroad engineer, quoted at the beginning of the chapter, was prophetic in his observation that learning is what most of us will be doing for a living in the 21st century. What Perlman did not know is that we would discover so much about ourselves and our capacity to learn, and that this learning would embody such awe-inspiring potential for HI.

2

A Fluid Workforce

"Finite players play within boundaries; infinite players play with boundaries."

—James P. Carse

We are amidst a paradigm shift in the nature of work. AI, automation, digital platforms, and other innovations are transforming businesses—from how organizations are managed to how they meet the needs of their customers. These innovations have the potential to contribute tremendously to economic growth, productivity, and quality of life for millions of people.

Robotics and other innovations are gaining in adoption and scope of use, increasingly assuming the tasks performed by people, such as warehouse picking or order-taking, and doing things humans cannot do, like parsing big data sets or making a precision computer chip en masse. These technologies are also transforming the workplace and the way we work. As a result, some occupations will decline, others will grow, and many more will evolve.

While technology is altering the business landscape, the COVID-19 pandemic has accelerated the digital or automation changes already underway in many companies and forced others with slow or no plans for automation to get on board to survive. The colliding of these two disruptions has caused a mass reallocation of work and loss of tens of thousands of jobs, resulting in layoffs in some industries, hiring in others, and a growing gig workforce. We've all experienced the result of these disruptions and maybe even contributed to the acceleration, with changes to our personal lives.

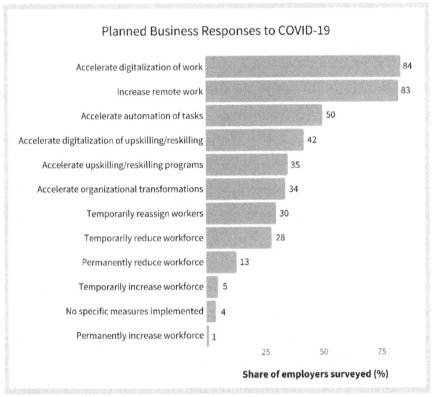

Adapting to Covid: Digitalization, upskilling/reskilling, and re-thinking traditional work processes (including remote work and company reorganization) were common themes in the 2020 Future of Jobs Survey.[29]

With concerns about face-to-face interaction in the age of the pandemic, we were spending more time in our homes than ever before. We were not in-store shopping, dining out, going to the movies, visiting family and friends, and traveling (for business or pleasure) with as much frequency. These changes in behavior increased the demand for conveniences such as grocery delivery, online retail shopping, and food delivery services, as well as for the comforts of home goods and home entertainment. Some of these new patterns of behavior continue to persist as the pandemic recedes.

While some businesses have benefited from the pandemic, others struggle to recover. Airlines, hotels, and car rental services reported record losses in 2020 in both profits and employees. The declines in dining, shopping, and entertainment outside of the home obliterated hundreds of thousands of jobs in the brick-and-mortar world, some of which may never come back.

Work life has changed dramatically as well. At the peak of the pandemic in the summer of 2020, 66 percent of U.S. employees were working remotely.[30] Companies invested in digital transformation initiatives to address gaps in cloud applications and cybersecurity. And remote-work technology platforms such as Zoom, Microsoft Teams, Adobe's PDF technology, and Docusign® took off and permanently changed how people and teams interact. While some workers have slowly started returning to the office, others choose to quit work altogether as they reassess their lives post-pandemic.[31]

And for those who lost or will lose their jobs—from busboys to financial analysts—and for college graduates not finding entry-level positions, being a free agent is sometimes the only option left until companies begin hiring again.

The Gig Economy

Tina Brown, former *New Yorker* editor and founder of *The Daily Beast*, coined the term "Gig Economy" in 2009. She describes how an expanding number of people today are piecing together a living through "a bunch of free-floating projects, consultancies, and part-time bits and pieces."[32]

Gig work is a familiar work life for those at the lower end of the income brackets, for the unemployed, for people who work part-time, or for those who work full-time and moonlight. But today, gig workers include the demographic that once assumed that a college degree, especially from an elite school, was the passport to job security. Since the start of the pandemic, it's likely that many professionals across many industries, who've become gig workers out of necessity, may not be going back to nine-to-five jobs anytime soon.

There is no universal definition of a "gig worker," making them a challenging demographic cohort to categorize and track through time. Moreover, the definition of what a "gig" is has expanded as digital technology has enabled more kinds of freelance work. The Bureau of Labor Statistics reported that in 2017, "workers in alternative arrangements," such as independent contractors and temporary workers, represented 10 percent of the total employed, with little change since 1995.[33]

According to Deloitte's 2018 Global Human Capital Trends study, more than 40 percent of workers in the U.S. are employed in alternative work engagements, such as contingent, part-time or gig work.[34] The Aspin Institute's "Future of Work" initiative estimated in December of 2020 that gig workers represented about 35 percent of the U.S. workforce, up from between 14 and 20 percent in 2014.[35] These figures are sure to grow as the pandemic gives reason for more and more companies to adopt digital technologies, automate what were once human-only tasks, and shift to hybrid work arrangements.

The Third Disruption

Colliding weather systems create storms of their own. Like a perfect storm, the double disruption brought on by technology and the pandemic has created a third disruption—an upheaval in the skills and capabilities people need to perform in this emerging human-machine work world.

The nature of work is changing. It is being enhanced by technology and will increasingly require complex and interpersonal skills like critical thinking skills and collaboration over routine task-based work. In some industries, such as warehousing and transportation, the work is shifting from *doing* the work to *overseeing* the work of automated systems and robots. Companies are experiencing epic shifts in their business models, causing a reduction in the need for specific skillsets and, as a result, the number of people required to perform the work. While much thought has been given to the repercussions, these converging disruptions require increasing attention to the capabilities of the human workforce.

There's been a growing belief among investors and CEOs that corporations need to be responsible for investing in their employees for the long-term versus thinking of them as a disposable or replaceable resource. In the pre-pandemic summer of 2019, the Business Roundtable, an association of over 180 CEOs of America's leading companies, pledged to invest in their workers in the face of automation. Given the disproportional impacts of automation on the poor and marginalized, the leaders acknowledged that it's just not possible to be sustainable in the long-term without an economy that "serves all Americans."[36]

Yet, amid the economic disruption in 2020, the decisions made by business leaders were still guided by the number one objective: maximize profitable returns for the shareholders. Between April and September 2020, one of the most unstable economic periods in modern history, 45 of the 50 largest publicly traded U.S. companies made a profit. Yet despite their success, half of those companies held layoffs in the same period, collectively cutting more than 100,000 workers from their workforces.[37]

Just a year earlier, many of the CEOs of the companies involved in those layoffs had signed the Business Roundtable pledge. True, the pandemic may have sidelined many promises, but the nearsightedness of maximizing profits must be met with some longer-term thinking about people and the changing nature of work. To maintain our sustainability well into the future, we must think of the boundaries of the game of business as fluid and consider the role of humans in work with an infinite mindset.

Finite or Infinite

Philosopher and religious scholar Dr. James P. Carse, who wrote *Finite and Infinite Games: A Vision of Life and Play*, reflected on the nature of play itself, especially play that saw no value in winning, or even play that actively avoided winning; a state of play he called "The Infinite Game."[38]

Carse observed that there are at least two kinds of games, finite and infinite. Finite games are played for the purpose of winning and involve a specific set of rules and boundaries. Think of a game of musical chairs, or chess, or a sports competition. The participants are determined ahead of time and compete until someone, or some team has won. At that point, the game ends.

Finite players see boundaries, and every move they make is within a boundary, what Carse calls a "phenomenon of opposition." Infinite players see a horizon, a "phenomenon of vision." Every move an infinite player makes is toward that horizon, knowing that they can't reach the horizon, but they *can* extend it.[39] Infinite games are played for the purpose of continuing the play. The rules are changeable, new players can join the game at any time, and the objective is to continue the game indefinitely.

Inspired by Carse's work, in his book, *The Infinite Game*, Simon Sinek added a new and unique dimension by applying an infinite mindset to the game of business. Sinek's realizations were that the more you look at the world through the lens of finite and infinite, the more you begin to see infinite games all around you, games with no finish lines and no winners, where all things are journeys and not events.[40]

In other words, there's no point at which the game is over, and the players shake hands and walk away. Instead, the game is constantly in flux, the rules change, and even the players change. The most telling illustration of flux and change is the list of companies that top the Fortune 500. At the onset of the 21st century, the top five companies were GM, Walmart, Exxon Mobil, Ford, and GE.[41] In 2021, the top five are Walmart, Amazon, Apple, CVS Health, and United HealthGroup.[42]

2000		2021	
COMPANY	REVENUE ($M)	COMPANY	REVENUE ($M)
1. General Motors	189,058	1. Walmart	559,151
2. Walmart	166,809	2. Amazon	386,064
3. Exxon Mobil	163,881	3. Apple	274,515
4. Ford Motor	162,558	4. CVS Health	268,706
5. General Electric	111,630	5. UnitedHealth Group	257,141
6. Intl. Business Machines	87,548	6. Berkshire Hathaway	245,510
7. CitiGroup	82,005	7. McKesson	231,051
8. AT&T	62,391	8. AmerisourceBergen	189,893.9
9. Altria Group	61,751	9. Alphabet	182,527
10. Boeing	57,993	10. Exxon Mobil	181,502

Fortune 500 Top 10 Companies: The largest corporations in the United States by total revenue, 2000 and 2021.[43,44]

Looking through the lens of an infinite mindset reveals just how much of the business landscape is a series of transformations and reincarnations. Netflix changed the rules of video rental, Airbnb changed the hotel service industry, and Uber adapted to the sharing economy, rendering the taxi archaic. The rules are changing, the players are changing, but the game goes on.

The problem with playing business as a finite game is that it is fundamentally short-sighted. When we play business as a finite game, it deprives us of innovation and creativity. It can also lead to suboptimal decision-making, particularly when those decisions are long-term and involve the long-term interests of customers and employees.

Consider how this game plays out in "the war for talent." The word itself, "war," implies winners and losers and an endpoint, which occurs presumably when a company wins and acquires that talent before someone else does. It also suggests a finite resource for which warring parties need to compete. Companies fighting a war for talent are investing huge sums of money every year to acquire and retain that talent. The problem with this thinking is that talent is not absolute. The rules of business are constantly changing, and players are in flux, so talent and the necessary skills to do the job are in flux.

Winning a talent war is fleeting then, and not winning at all. When you look through the finite/infinite lens, what starts to come into focus is that companies engaged in fighting a war for talent are playing the wrong game. Talent—and in particular, people—is not a zero-sum game.

Development as an Infinite Game

What would companies do differently if they looked at talent as an infinite game? Consider AT&T. The company has one of the largest workforces in the world at 250,000 employees.

Internal skills analysis revealed that only half of its employees had the necessary science, technology, engineering, and math skills the company required. Furthermore, 100,000 employees were in jobs involving functions that the company predicts won't exist within ten years.[45]

This discovery presented AT&T with two options: hire software and engineering people (expensive and inadequate in the long run) or reskill their existing workforce so they could be competent in the technology and build the skills required to run the business going forward.

In response, AT&T launched "Future Ready," a $1 billion reskilling initiative that includes online courses: collaborations with Coursera, Udacity, and leading universities. In its first year, over 180,000 employees participated in its Future Ready program. Employees can assess their skills, then pursue short-term badges, nanodegrees that take up to a year to complete, or master's degrees in fields like computer science and data science offered in partnership with institutions such as the Georgia Institute of Technology and the University of Notre Dame.[46]

In 2018, McDonald's Corporation invested $150 million to fund its five-year global "Archways to Opportunity" education program for the company's 400,000 U.S. restaurant employees. Initially available to employees after nine months of employment, McDonald's lowered the eligibility requirement to 90 days, the equivalent of a summer job. And the company extended education benefits to restaurant employees' family members to earn a high school diploma, receive upfront college tuition assistance, access free education advising services, or learn English as a second language.[47]

McDonald's restaurant staff and their families have a choice for how they use the tuition grant—whether for a community college, four-year university, or trade school. There's no time limit on tuition assistance, and employees and family members will be able to pursue their education and career interests at their own pace.

Amazon announced in 2019 the plan to spend more than $700 million to train 100,000 employees for higher-skilled jobs over the next six years. Dubbed "Upskilling 2025," Amazon offers development opportunities to employees to pursue roles in information technology, such as data technician, software engineer, or cloud computing services.[48] More recently, as the pandemic continued to upend careers, Amazon announced a broader global upskilling initiative aimed at helping 29 million people retrain by 2025, equipping them with cloud-computing skills.[49]

Other companies are expanding their education benefits as well. In 2021, both Walmart[50] and Target[51] announced that they would pay 100% of expenses for their combined nearly 1.9 million frontline store employees, including part-time employees. Both companies are working with Guild, which is, according to their website, an education platform that upskills workers and helps prepare organizations for the future.[52]

Cultivating a resilient talent pool for the future will require that employers continue to develop their people and that employees bring ongoing skill development into their work. In effect, we are all players in an infinite game. And if we want to stay in the game, we have only one choice: to be agile and fluid as the work demands.

Fluid Workforce

Accenture coined the term "Liquid Workforce" in 2016 to describe the use of a flexible and adaptable workforce composed of project-oriented working groups of agile employees and gig workers, including contractors and freelancers.[53] Given that work will change continually, a "liquid" workforce enables companies to adapt, develop and access necessary skills more quickly.

I prefer the term "fluid" to describe a flexible and agile workforce. After all, a liquid is merely a phase of matter, while fluid is a form of matter that "can flow from one place to another through any opening without showing any traits of rigidity."[54] While employees will have more flexibility to go where the work is needed, they will need to update their skills frequently to stay relevant. This means that to have a fluid workforce, companies will need systems in place to re-skill and move workers continually and have access to gig workers.

One type of fluid workforce is powered by a new way of structuring an organization known as "holacracy." According to Holacracy One, a holacracy consultancy,

> "A holacracy is a way of structuring and running your organization that replaces the conventional management hierarchy. Instead of operating top-down, power is distributed throughout the organization—giving individuals and teams freedom

while staying aligned to the organization's purpose....Authority and decision making are distributed among fluid 'circles'..."[55]

Invented by Brian Robertson in 2007 and popularized by Zappos, an important aspect of holacracy is that it is essentially an "internal gig economy." In traditional organizations, an employee is hired to do a job, and it's often difficult for people to shape their roles or switch jobs. In holacracies, individuals have several roles which they craft and revise to address shifting organizational and individual needs and skills.

With ongoing changes in the skills required to do work, the 4IR has driven companies to build internal talent marketplaces to support internal gig-like workforces. As more workers move to working remotely and more offices are shuttering their doors, the pandemic has accelerated this trend. According to Gloat®, a company that helps organizations "democratize career development" and build internal marketplaces, it's easier to find a job outside of your company than within.

Internal talent marketplaces allow the most efficient means of matching individual capabilities with organizational goals. Consider a situation where you have 60 percent of skill overlap with an entirely new field. You could, as an employee, develop those skills to qualify yourself for the job and possibly even develop some of those skills on the job. For companies, this enables access to hidden talent and means not having to look outside the organization for more expensive talent externally.

Josh Bersin, founder of Bersin & Associates, now Bersin by Deloitte, notes that companies have been working to improve internal talent mobility since 2015. Not only does it save money on recruiting and increase engagement, it also enables companies to find internal expertise and create a strong sense of belonging in their workforce. Bersin believes an internal talent marketplace serves a two-fold purpose:[56]

1. Creates an efficient internal gig economy within the organization
2. Drives learning through ongoing stretch and rotational opportunities

An example of a company with an internal talent marketplace is Unilever. Unilever launched an AI-powered internal talent marketplace, Gloat, to create opportunities for employees to continually transform themselves through learning. By accessing the platform, Unilever employees can work on projects for a small or large proportion of time, increasing the depth of their expertise of a current skill or building new skills and experiences.[57]

Considering the double disruption, the need to build Human Intelligence (HI) is of critical importance to maintain play in the infinite game. Perhaps Larry Fink, CEO of BlackRock, understands the infinite game better than anyone. In his 2021 letter to CEOs, Fink wrote: *"BlackRock is a fiduciary to our clients, helping them invest for long-term goals."*[58]

Fink recognizes the greater responsibility companies have to their communities, employees, and society as a whole. Appreciating this and the power BlackRock wields as the world's largest institutional investor, Fink single-handedly has driven a seismic shift in the way American companies think about sustainability and climate change, driving many to adopt net-zero emissions pledges.

Fink also recognizes the greater responsibility companies have to communities and employees and their responsibility to address racial injustice and economic inequality issues. In his 2021 letter, he wrote that in 2020 "purposeful companies, with better environmental, social, and governance (ESG) profiles, have outperformed their peers."[59]

Building skills among poor and marginalized communities in the U.S. and abroad is critical to addressing these inequities, exacerbated by automation and the pandemic. Companies must take collective responsibility for developing and re-skilling workers to ensure the sustainability of our communities if the game will truly be infinite.

Resilient Workforce

According to the World Economic Forum (WEF), "developing and enhancing human skills and capabilities through education, learning, and meaningful work are key drivers of economic success, of individual well-being and societal cohesion."[60] The WEF has been tracking demand for cross-functional skills since 2016. Of the skills identified as most critical on the 2020 Future of Jobs report, *Active Learning and Learning Strategies* is number two. We must be better learners if we are to thrive in the new world of work.

In addition to strengthening key skills, success in the future will require a sort of *grounded optimism*. When I think of grounded optimism, I think of the Stockdale Paradox developed by Jim Collins in his book *Good to Great*. The paradox is named after Admiral Jim Stockdale who was the highest-ranking military officer in the "Hanoi Hilton" prisoner-of-war camp during the height of the Vietnam War. Stockdale maintained an unwavering belief in freedom for his fellow prisoners and himself while at the same time accepting the brutal facts of their reality.[61]

The Stockdale Paradox exposes that while optimism is important in being resilient, that optimism cannot be untethered from reality. This is the very essence of why learning is so critical now. The world of work is undergoing a fundamental transformation, and while optimism of our ability to transform during change is critical, it's important to understand the stark reality that the status quo won't help us. We will need to be agile and continually anticipate and develop new and stronger skillsets.

Luckily, we can weather this challenge by embracing our own human capability to learn. Resilience is a muscle strengthened through learning, and becoming a learner increases one's resolve. The more you know, the farther you can go, which is compounded by the mental fortitude learning develops.

Part 2

The Art and Science of Learning

3
Thinking About Learning

"Thinking about thinking has to be a principal ingredient of any empowering practice of education."

—Jerome Bruner

Remember the person in your high school or college class who didn't necessarily have the highest IQ or test scores but often had the highest grades? If they were smart about anything, it was about how to learn. They thought about thinking and discovered how to leverage a range of strategies to memorize, synthesize, and problem-solve.

What's more, they understood when they knew something and when they didn't, or when a particular type of knowledge was more difficult to learn than another. They had a high degree of *metacognition*, i.e., they were aware of their own thinking and learning processes.

I remember having an awareness and understanding of my own thinking and learning processes around the age of twelve—metacognition in how I synthesized information and formulated ideas. In fact, later in life, when I began learning about strategies and tactics for learning, I recognized that I had already established many of those plans and approaches on my own. For example, I spread out study time rather than cramming for a test, and I tried to associate new learning with things I already knew so I could more easily remember the information. I reflected on what worked and what didn't and developed different learning strategies.

One of the key findings of The National Academy of Sciences' synthesis of research on the science of learning is the effectiveness of a metacognitive approach to learning—that learning how to learn is the key to developing new skills and increasing knowledge.[62]

Over the past two hundred years, researchers from different fields have advanced many theories to explain how humans and other animal species acquire, organize, and deploy knowledge and skills. The result is a gradual confluence of understanding that has significantly advanced our ability to learn over time. Additionally, we now know that humans are born to learn, and our capacity to learn exceeds that of any other species.[63]

These older and essentially intuitive learning theories are now supported by research conducted using brain-imaging technologies such as functional magnetic resonance imaging (fMRI) developed around 1990.[64] Chapter 5 will focus entirely on these and other discoveries and how we as humans are hardwired to learn.

This chapter traces the origins of our ideas about learning, how leading psychologists, philosophers, educators, and other scientists have applied those ideas, and how the evolution of those theories of learning over the past several hundred years has deepened our knowledge about ourselves and how we learn. Through understanding these insights, even a little, you can enhance your metacognition and your own ability to develop and grow.

A History of Learning

The *Encyclopedia of the Science of Learning* defines *learning* as a relatively permanent change in behavior and/or in mental associations due to experience.[65] I like to think of learning more specifically as a change in one's brain (*knowledge, mindset, or behavior*) resulting from one's experience. This process is inherently unique to each individual and their own schemata, that is, the patterns and cognitive structures of their unique experiences and knowledge.

The study of human learning has a rich history that spans philosophy, psychology, anthropology, education, sociology, computer science, and neuroscience. Until technology in the 1990s enabled us to peer deeper into the brain and understand its physiology and impact on learning, the disciplines of philosophy first, then psychology, had influenced and controlled learning and education for generations.

Before the 19th Century

Long before James Ferrier (1808-1864) coined the term *epistemology* to describe the study of knowledge, the study originated in philosophy, and philosophers contemplated the nature, origin, and scope of knowledge and rationality.[66] The word epistemology comes from the Greek words "episteme" and "logos." Episteme can be translated as "knowledge" or "understanding" while logos can be translated as "argument" or "reason."[67]

Plato (c. 427–c. 347 BC) believed that the soul is eternal, and knowledge is innate, i.e., we already know everything we need to know. Plato's epistemology, founded on learnings from dialogues with his teacher Socrates, was an attempt to understand what it is to know. His *Doctrine of Recollection*, with Socrates as his mouthpiece, was among the first to present a theory of learning. Plato and Socrates believed that everything is already known and that learning is the development of ideas buried deep in the soul as a means of recollecting that knowledge. Thus, when an idea is learned, it is simply being recalled from deep in the annals of our eternal memories.[68]

Later, Aristotle (384-322 BC) viewed education through the lens of reason and habit. He proposed that anything that we must learn to do, we learn best by doing it. Such learning is complemented by reason, which involves understanding "the causes of things."[69] Like Plato, Aristotle considered learning a continuous practice occurring throughout one's life, although at different degrees at different ages.

Fast forward 1,500 years through the Dark Ages and the bubonic plague pandemic, and we're brought to the Renaissance and the rebirth of European culture, art, and science. The individual as artist and scientist starts to take prominence, and we begin to challenge past beliefs that knowledge is innate and not acquired. We start to build on our understanding of ourselves.

Thomas Aquinas (1225-1274), a medieval Catholic priest at the onset of the re-awakening, was influenced by Aristotle's teachings and based much of his philosophy and work on his study of Aristotle's works. Like Aristotle, Aquinas recognized different kinds of knowledge, such as sensory knowledge—a cumulative ability to learn from sight, sound, touch, movement, smell, and taste. Sensory knowledge also includes learning from internal sensory experiences such as pleasure, hunger, thirst, or distress.[70]

Rene Descartes (1596-1650) spent his life absorbed in the study of metaphysics and mathematics. According to Descartes, *"Knowledge is conviction based on a reason so strong that it can never be shaken by a stronger reason."*[71] Descartes believed that the pursuit of knowledge required the pursuit of convictions, and the first and most significant "certainty" obtained through this process is the existence of the self, reflected in his philosophical assertion, *"I think; therefore, I am."*[72]

Descartes believed that learning is a personal journey made up of external experiences and internal thoughts. According to Descartes, everyone is responsible for their own questioning of truths. Therefore, each person is ultimately their own teacher.[73]

John Locke's (1632-1704) views on education were based on his pragmatic theory of human knowledge explained in his work, *An Essay Concerning Human Understanding*. Here he advances the idea that education means rigorously shaping knowledge according to each person's nature and abilities.[74]

Locke was one of the first philosophers to reject the notion that certain kinds of knowledge are imprinted on the human mind at birth, such as a knowledge of the existence of God, or certain moral truths, or of the laws of logic or mathematics. This belief in innate ideas had its origins with Plato, who was a powerfully influencing force for more than a thousand years after his death. Locke influenced our moving beyond those fixed beliefs and opened our minds to a greater understanding of ourselves. He argued that an idea could not be said to be "in the mind" until the person is conscious of it.[75]

The following century represented a period of great activity in reformulating educational principles. Although teaching methods remained geared toward textbook memorization and strict discipline, educators were in line with the belief that a child's nature should be the starting point of education.[76]

By the end of the 18th century, we saw a shift from philosophy to psychology as the guiding discipline for learning and education. This meant that education programs should be child-centered and not subject-centered, and the stages of education must be related to the stages of child development. This new line of reasoning made learning more dynamic and less rigid.

Learning in the 19th Century

German psychologist Hermann Ebbinghaus (1850-1909) became the first in his field to study learning and memory systematically by carrying out long, exhausting memory experiments on himself. His concentration was on the strength and durability of memory. He was the first to describe what later became known as *the forgetting curve*, illustrating the decline of memory retention over time.[77]

William James (1842-1910), often considered the father of American psychology of education, established the first course in psychology in 1887 at Harvard University. He's also credited with establishing the psychological movement, *functionalism*, an understanding of the biological processes behind and purpose of human consciousness.[78] James's work focused on mental activities such as perception, memory, and feeling, but his passion was the art of teaching children. He saw the student as a dynamic being, not just a mind to fill but a complex and growing organism.[79]

The contribution of these and other prominent figures in philosophy and psychology in the late 1800s advanced our knowledge of ourselves and how we learn, and laid the groundwork for psychology as being the guiding discipline for learning and education in the 20th century.

Learning in the 20th Century

Simultaneous—and sometimes conflicting—social and intellectual movements shaped American education in the 20th century. Against this backdrop, many theoretical frameworks about learning emerged in psychology, shaping how we learn, from acquiring knowledge through repetition to building understanding through discovery and experimentation. Three of these frameworks stand out as particularly influential: behaviorism, cognitivism, and constructivism.

As we trace the origins of these three learning structures, keep in mind the patterns of the second and third industrial revolutions and try to note the parallel evolution of these theories—from rapid standardization and industrialization to decentralization and accessibility of information.

"Class, repeat after me...."

Behavioral learning theory, also known as *behaviorism,* involves acquiring knowledge or behavioral responses from experience. Behaviorists view learning as "conditioning" or habituation through response to a given environmental stimulus. Behavioral learning theory views learners as passive participants in the learning process who can be studied in an observable manner.

In this process, teachers show students how they should react and respond to certain stimuli. Positive reinforcement, such as earning a gold star for spelling a word correctly or an A on an exam, helps sustain that behavior. Negative reinforcement, or the removal of an unpleasant stimulus, also serves as a reward to encourage learning. (This is often confused with punishment, in which the learner is penalized for the failure to learn). The key to learning in the behavioral paradigm is the stimulus-response repetition, causing a lasting change in behavior.

Much of behavioral learning theory has been based primarily on studies of animal behavior. As you might know, if you've ever taken psychology 101, Russian physiologist Ivan Pavlov (1849-1936) conducted one of the most defining studies in behavioral psychology through a series of experiments with dogs smelling food and producing saliva in anticipation of feeding. His research would become renowned for demonstrating how *classical conditioning* could be used to create an association between the occurrence of one event in anticipation of another.[80] Pavlov's studies were the classic behaviorist paradigm.

American psychologist Edward Thorndike (1874-1949) built on Pavlov's research and founded the theory of connectivism, which states that behavioral responses to specific stimuli are established through a process of trial and error and establishing neural connections between the stimuli and the most satisfying responses.[81] Today, the idea of association is virtually common sense. Thanks, Thorndike.

His research didn't stop there. Thorndike's "Law of Effect" states that any behavior that is followed by favorable results is likely to be repeated, and any behavior followed by unfavorable results is likely to end. This basic finding would later serve as the foundation for operant conditioning, which differs from Pavlov's classical conditioning in that it involves learning from the consequences of a behavior.[82]

John B. Watson (1878-1958) and B.F. Skinner (1904-1990), two acclaimed American psychologists, focused on the role of environmental factors in shaping the intelligence of the child. They believed that environmental interactions dictated an infant's growth and outcome instead of stable predictors such as genetics. Like Pavlov, they viewed students as passive participants in learning; but they further argued that a child is malleable, with the ability to learn through positive and negative reinforcement.[83]

The rise of behaviorism is reflective of its time in history when people were adapting to urban life in a mechanized world. While behaviorism is outdated as a sole method of teaching, conditioning strategies are effectively employed in implicit, unconscious learning, like learning to write or ride a bike, where repetition and practice are key to developing a habit-like response to a given stimulus.

Conditioning strategies can also be used any time we want to develop a new habit or motor skill. Our world is filled with examples of positive and negative reinforcements. The design of passive restraint systems in vehicles forces you to buckle your seatbelt to stop the annoying beeping sound (negative reinforcement). You might reward yourself with a small treat after going to the gym as a means of positive reinforcement.

Cognitivism

Since the 1950s, most of what we know as "the science of learning" comes from the field of cognitive psychology. The cognitive revolution presented a new paradigm that was in stark contrast to behavioral psychology. Cognitivism is a school of thought which emphasizes the mental process of thinking and experiencing. Unlike behaviorism, cognitivism is concerned with complex reasoning mechanisms and information processing, such as language, problem-solving, decision-making, and judgment.[84] In this school of thought, the learner is an active participant in the acquisition of knowledge.

Cognitive learning theory is primarily concerned with how new information is assimilated into existing mental maps or schemata. Sir Frederic Bartlett (1886–1969) first introduced the concept of schema—a cognitive structure that helps us organize information. We use schemata collectively to help interpret the world and guide our behavior. Since Bartlett's concept was introduced, many researchers have expounded on the construct. Carefully consider the following sentence and see if you can understand it's meaning:

As nt wht ur contry cn do for you—ask wht y cn d fr ur contry.

Most likely, you can discern the sentence: *"Ask not what your country can do for you—ask what you can do for your country."* That is because you have a mental map, or schema, for the English language, and you can discern what the sentence is trying to say. If you are familiar with that sentence from John F. Kennedy's 1961 inaugural address, you may have been able to figure out that sentence even more quickly, drawing on that mental category of information. Further, that mental map may have reminded you explicitly of something else, like a story about your mother volunteering after hearing President Kennedy's inaugural speech.

If I told you that a Violetear is a bird, you immediately begin to formulate conclusions about the bird based on existing schemata. You know birds fly, they have beaks and eat seeds and insects. You might even conclude the bird has violet coloring of some sort. If I told you the Violetear is a type of hummingbird, you begin to mentally reference other categories of information and draw additional inferences, like *this bird probably consumes nectar*. Learning is a process of building on and modifying mental schemata—through analogies, hierarchies, and categorizations—to help learners acquire new knowledge.

Jean Piaget (1896-1980) was a key figure in 20th-century developmental psychology. He was a cognitivist who developed theories of constructivism and gained much attention and notoriety for his theory of cognitive development. He describes the four stages of cognitive development that children attain as they grow from infancy to adolescence.[85] Piaget recognized this as occurring through progressive stages, with each stage being foundational to the next.[86]

At any age, children rely on their current cognitive structures to understand the world around them. Piaget viewed intellectual development as a process in which children continually reconstruct thoughts formed at earlier levels using higher-order concepts through accommodation and assimilation of their current cognitive schemata.[87] In this process, children may interpret and respond to the same concepts and events in very different ways because cognitive schemata evolve and take different shapes through different life stages and experiences.[88]

Piaget's work formed the basis for much of what we knew about developmental psychology through to the end of the 20th century, informing many of our theories and instructional approaches. For example, Piaget discovered that we could more easily learn new information when we connect it to what we already know by mapping it to existing mental structures. Human Intelligence (HI) then is a continual process of encoding new information and reorganizing existing schemata.

Jerome Bruner (1915-2016), an influential cognitive scientist, studied how an individual's unique needs and motivations affect their perception and, ultimately, their learning process.

His theories focus on culture as a key influence on each individual's specific development pattern and present a broader framework of our schemata. He argued that culture embodies *"a set of values, skills and ways of life"* and becomes a key part of *"sense-making."*[89]

Unlike Piaget, Bruner believed that even young children could learn complex concepts with the right support, and he applied this thinking to approaches to education. Bruner later developed a theory of education that expanded our learning and development frontiers.[90]

Cognitivism and Constructivism

Piaget's and Bruner's theories set the stage for constructivist approaches to teaching and learning in the 20th century. While Piaget recognized human knowledge as a reflection of our inner thoughts and external information, Bruner saw learning as necessarily embedded in culture. Through the lens of constructivism, individuals build their own meaning. Development then is a deeply personal and unique experience.

While cognitivism focuses on the instructor imparting knowledge or skills, constructivist classrooms encourage students to develop new knowledge or meaning on their own. According to Bruner, individuals are not receptacles where teachers merely fill a vessel. Moreover, facts are not immutable and cultural context is constantly evolving. The aim of education then is to create autonomous, self-directed learners.

Constructivist theorists like Bruner and others transformed the way we think about education, paving the way for progressive changes to educational systems. Shifting away from the view of learning as mechanistic assimilation to that of discovering and creating new knowledge changed our cultural mindset and provided a foundation for new opportunities.

A Layering of Knowledge

Over the last two centuries, various practitioners and scientists have continually elaborated on our understanding of how humans learn. While we have distilled many of these theories into practical applications (which we will explore in the subsequent chapters), we might take it a step further and broadly view the collection of theories, not in juxtaposition to one another, but as a layering of schemata foundational to metacognition. By exploring these patterns, we can improve our ability to think about thinking.

Nobel Laureate Economist Herbert Simon once said,

> "It should not be supposed that every advance in human knowledge increases the amount of information that has to be mastered by professionals. On the contrary some of the most important progress in science is the discovery and testing of powerful new theories that allow large numbers of facts to be subsumed under a few general principles. There is a constant competition between the elaboration of knowledge and its compression into more parsimonious form by theories."[91]

In other words, sometimes big ideas encapsulate years of research and knowledge.

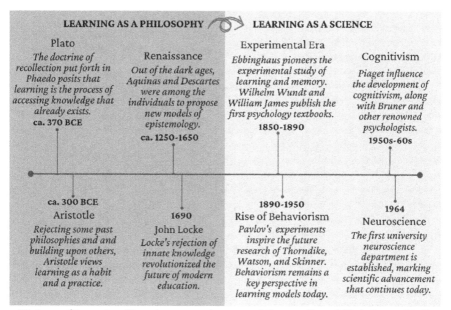

History of Learning: These key moments represent the paradigm shifts in humankind's study of learning.

You might have noticed that our understanding of how we learn has accelerated throughout history. Most of what we previously knew about learning occurred in the last two hundred years. However, in the past twenty years, with advances in neuroscience, we have learned significantly more about ourselves and how we learn than in the last two hundred. With the double disruption of the 4IR as the backdrop, science has accelerated our understanding of human knowledge and development, providing unparalleled opportunity to uncover mysteries of human learning that could propel our abilities to learn and develop new capabilities.

We will look at recent developments in Chapter 5, where I explore neuroscience. But first, let's look at common myths about learning that we need to let go of in order to advance our ability to learn.

4

Exposing the Myths

"It is what we know already that often prevents us from learning."

—Claude Bernard

In the 1980s and 90s, the diet trend of the time was "low-fat." Scientific studies at that time showed a correlation between high-fat diets and high cholesterol levels, suggesting that reducing dietary fat was the critical component in the battle to lose weight and prevent heart disease.

As early as 1977, the U.S. Department of Health and Human Services began urging Americans to eat less fat, an effort promoted by both physicians and the federal government. The food industry responded with low-fat products, and many Americans, swept up in the trend, adopted low-fat diets, even though there was no clear evidence that they prevented heart disease or promoted weight loss.[92]

Physicians, health magazines, the news media, and health organizations all got on board and propagated the low-fat ideology. In 1988, The American Heart Association (AHA) introduced its program to label foods with its "heart healthy" seal of approval. Food companies were more than willing to pay the AHA to have their food products approved and stamped with the familiar symbol heart with a white checkmark on it.[93]

By 1997, fifty-five major food companies participated with over 600 products certified as "heart-healthy." Many were children's cereal products and snacks, including Kellogg's Frosted Flakes, Fruity Marshmallow Krispies, and Low-Fat Pop-Tarts.[94] The low-fat philosophy had taken such a hold on society that sugar-laden, refined, processed foods had qualified for AHA approval as heart-healthy.[95]

The food industry began replacing fat with sugar in processed foods, leading to what we knew in the 1990s as the "SnackWell's Phenomenon" (named after Nabisco's SnackWell cookies).[96]

While the low-fat approach was achieving ideological status among the American medical community, advertisers, and the media, Americans overall in the 1990s were getting fatter, leading to what many called an "obesity epidemic." The obesity rate in the population considerably increased from 12 percent in 1991 to 17.9 percent in 1998.[97] What we didn't realize at the time was that you can get fat and sick from eating too much sugar and too many carbohydrates.

In 2002, *The New York Times Magazine* published Gary Taubes's explosive article, "What if it's all been a big fat lie?"[98] exposing the low-fat myth and pointing to studies that showed that eating less fat and more carbohydrates were directly linked to obesity. Moreover, recent science suggests that low-sugar or low-carb diets yield promising results regarding weight loss and cardiovascular health (such as blood pressure and triglyceride levels),[99] with low-carb being significantly more effective than low-fat when compared directly.[100] Meanwhile, low-fat labeling is shown to provoke calorie underestimation and therefore increased consumption.[101]

In 2013, the AHA significantly tightened its guidelines for what they certify as "Heart-Healthy." Yet, many carbohydrate-laden packaged foods continue to be marketed as heart-healthy *without* the AHA checkmark. This example shows a side-by-side comparison of the nutritional facts and ingredients for an original baking mix and the same mix as a "heart smart" recipe. As you can see, there's very little difference between the two (differences in the US Recommended Daily Allowances for fat, sugar, and sodium are 1%; the heart smart recipe has an additional gram of sugar).

Nutrition Facts

Serving Size	1/3 cup mix (40g)
Amount Per Serving As Packaged	
Calories	**150**
	% Daily Value
Total Fat 3g	4%
Saturated Fat 1g	6%
Trans Fat 0g	
Cholesterol 0mg	0%
Sodium 380mg	16%
Total Carbohydrate 28g	10%
Dietary Fiber 1g	4%
Total Sugars 2g	
Incl. 2g Added Sugars	4%
Protein 3g	
Calcium 60mg	4%
Iron 1.4mg	8%
Not a significant source of Vitamin D and Potassium	

Nutrition Facts

Serving Size	1/3 cup mix (40g)
Amount Per Serving As Packaged	
Calories	**140**
	% Daily Value
Total Fat 2.5g	3%
Saturated Fat 0g	0%
Trans Fat 0g	
Polyunsaturated Fat 0.5g	
Monounsaturated Fat 1.5g	
Cholesterol 0mg	0%
Sodium 340mg	15%
Total Carbohydrate 27g	10%
Dietary Fiber < 1g	3%
Total Sugars 3g	
Incl. 2g Added Sugars	4%
Protein 3g	
Calcium 220mg	15%
Iron 1.5mg	8%
Not a significant source of Vitamin D and Potassium	

Heart Healthy Nutrition Label: Compare the original product on the left with the "Heart Healthy" version on the right, and you'll find little evidence to back up the marketing. [102, 103]

I share this because we, as a society, tend to perpetuate myths. Evidence shows that people continue to buy into the story because food is still sold as "heart smart," primarily because of its low-fat content (but without the AHA certification).

Another important insight is that knowledge and facts are not absolute, and the awareness and process of unlearning is just as important as learning itself. As we hold onto what we know, we sometimes miss new information. For example, the AHA rewrote its guidelines around what it considered heart-healthy on January 1, 2014.[104] Many people still adhere to the low-fat myth despite new scientific evidence and guidelines. Their adherence is detrimental to our collective health. Distortions about learning and the human capacity to learn can be equally detrimental to our collective intelligence.

We've been steadily growing in our knowledge of ourselves over the last 200 years, and we've learned a great deal about learning and education along the way. Yet, regardless of how much our intelligence has grown, we're still hindered by myths about our *ability* to learn—illusions that permeate our school and workplaces.

Four myths are getting in the way of living into both our individual and collective capacity to learn:

1. Intelligence—and who we are—is fixed.

2. People have different learning styles.

3. The same learning strategies that got us here will get us there.

4. We stop learning as adults, or it's too late to learn.

These misguided beliefs about ourselves and others have become so prevalent in our culture that they're embedded in our assessment of human capacity and resilience. These limiting beliefs keep many of us—young and old alike—from opening doors to our unlimited potential to learn and grow. They also can work to intensify inequality, something that I explore within the myths.

Exposing the myths, especially now in the face of new scientific evidence in brain physiology that I'll share in Chapter 5, will shed new light on old assumptions and increase the awareness needed to lift the barriers to our innate potential to learn.

Myth #1: Intelligence—and Who We Are—Is Fixed.

The 1983 satirical comedy *Trading Places* illustrates this first myth that intelligence is fixed and immutable.[105] The film tells the story of two wealthy financiers who make a one-dollar bet on whether nature or nurture is the determinant factor in the outcome of an individual's life. Is success a result of a person's innate character and abilities or a result of their environment and circumstance?

The lives of an upper-class commodities broker (Aykroyd) and a poor street hustler (Murphy) cross when they are unwittingly made the subject of this elaborate bet to test how each man will perform when their life circumstances are swapped. Murphy quickly disproves the overwhelmingly popular belief that, because of his background, he might not be "smart enough," while Aykroyd quickly debunks the myth of meritocracy. Self-limiting beliefs such as *"I'm not good at this"* or *"I'm not smart enough"* are borne from the myth that you are who you are and your intelligence is fixed. Included is the belief that some people are endowed from birth with more intelligence, while others go through life with less.

Not surprisingly, wealth confers what appears to be an undeniable advantage when it comes to having and acquiring intelligence. Neuroscientist and pediatrician Kimberly Noble studied 1,000 children from diverse backgrounds—including different geographical locations, races, ages, and genders—and found only one factor associated with higher brain cortical surface area: family income.[106]

The cerebral cortex is the part of the brain responsible for many higher-order brain functions such as sensation, perception, association, thought, memory, and physical action. The more folds there are in this area of the brain, the larger the surface area.[107] Dr. Noble found that those children in higher-income families, on average, had essentially larger cerebral cortexes. The resulting differences in cognitive function due to the difference in cortical surface area were seen as early as age two or three.[108]

In addition to providing a "head start" in brain surface area, wealth affords families the opportunity to send their children to schools with more resources and activities that challenge and stimulate their thinking processes, enabling them to learn more and ultimately achieve more. Take, for example, New Trier High School in Winnetka, Illinois—one of the wealthiest school districts in the United States. New Trier has some of the best educators in the country on its faculty and is known for its scholastic rigor. Outside of academics, the school offers opportunities that are not available at most high schools. It maintains over 150 clubs and activities that receive steady funding, 22 of which are varsity sports, including a bass fishing team and a ski troupe.[109]

Even if a child is not from a wealthy household, our educational system has conferred additional advantages to those identified as intelligent by doubling down on signs of cognitive ability early in their lives. Children seen as exceptionally bright may have other benefits of individualized development, improved school options, and opportunities to enroll in specialized education.

The result of these differences often causes some to believe they are better or worse off than their peers in other social groups when it comes to intelligence. Researchers Claude Steele and Joshua Aronson call this phenomenon "Stereotype Threat," which they define as *"…the risk of confirming, as self-characteristic, a negative stereotype about one's group."*[110] In other words, individuals of certain groups may believe they are inherently less capable and underperform on tests solely because of this self-limiting belief.

Steele and Aronson's studies focused on African American students. When prompted to reflect on a racial stereotype about their intellectual abilities, black test-takers tended to underperform on tests compared with white test-takers. Essentially, priming students with the thinking that their group tended to underperform on the test resulted in the group underperforming.[111] This same result did not occur in the control tests where black test-takers were not "primed" to believe they were less apt to perform well on the test.

Other researchers have pointed to other stereotypes, such as gender-based typecasts about which sex is better at math. According to a study by University of Washington researchers, children express the stereotype that math is for boys, not girls, as early as the second grade.[112]

Indeed, it's worth investing in, encouraging, and supporting our children's learning to the height of their capacity to learn. What holds us back are our assumptions, which often label some people as less intelligent. The question we should ask is what this kind of thinking engenders in the minds of those who might be asking, *"Why try?"*

"The Brain is Not Destiny"

Dr. Noble learned something in her studies of children's brains, namely that a child living in poverty is likely to have cognitive scores that are, on average, 60 percent lower than a child born into more fortunate circumstances. A poverty-born child is also five times more likely to drop out of high school. If the child does graduate high school, she'll be less likely to earn a college degree. And by the time she is 35 years old, if she spent her entire childhood living in poverty, she is up to 75 times more likely to be poor herself.[113]

But Noble believes it doesn't have to be that way.

> *"As a neuroscientist, one of the things I find most exciting about the human brain is that our experiences change our brains. Now, this concept, known as neuroplasticity, means that these differences in children's brain structure don't doom a child to a life*

of low achievement. The brain is not destiny. And if a child's brain can be changed, then anything is possible."[114]

You will learn in the next chapter about recent advances in neuroscience that have revealed that the human brain is far more malleable than we ever thought possible and how our experiences can actually modify our brain structure and function.

None of us are "destined" based on our cortical brain size, whether at age 2, 12, 30, or 50. From the third week of gestation through to old age, our brains are constantly changing and adapting, developing new neural pathways, and growing new brain cells.[115]

Mind Over Gray Matter

In the 1980s, Carol Dweck and her colleagues became interested in students' attitudes about failure. The team of researchers noticed that some students recovered while other students seemed devastated by even the smallest setbacks. After studying the behavior of thousands of children, Dr. Dweck created the terms "fixed mindset" and "growth mindset" to describe the polar attitudes people have about learning and intelligence.[116]

People with *fixed mindsets*—those who believe that abilities are fixed—are less likely to adapt and thrive in a changing environment than people with *growth mindsets*—those who believe that abilities can be developed. After decades of research, Dweck discovered the power of one's mindset and how success in almost every area of human effort can be dramatically influenced by what we think about ourselves and how we view our talents and abilities.[117]

You learned earlier about the phenomenon of "stereotype threat" and how African American college students can emulate the vulnerability and succumb to the racial stereotype, and as a result, underperform on tests compared to whites. Researchers also conducted an experiment to test an approach designed to help students resist stereotype threats. Students in the experimental condition group were encouraged to view "intelligence" as a flexible rather than fixed capacity in people. The researchers theorized that this encouraging thinking would engage the students in their studies and that they would feel less vulnerable—both of which could help boost their college grades.[118]

The results were consistent with the researchers' expectations. The black students (and, to some degree, the white students in the group), having been encouraged to view intelligence as malleable, reported a greater commitment to learning and received higher grade point averages than their counterparts in the two other control groups.[119]

Myth #2: People Have Different Learning Styles.

The fields of psychology and education were forever changed almost 40 years ago when psychologist Howard Gardner published his 1983 book, *Frames of Mind: The Theory of Multiple Intelligences*. His work detailed a new model of human intelligence that went beyond the traditional view of a single intelligence measured by standardized tests.[120]

Gardner's theory initially listed seven intelligences that work together: linguistic, logical-mathematical, musical, bodily-kinesthetic, spatial, interpersonal, and intrapersonal. He later added an eighth, naturalist intelligence, with the indication that there may be a few more.[121]

The theory became quite popular and widely adopted globally by K-12 and primary school educators looking for ways to reach students who didn't respond to traditional learning approaches. Over time, "multiple intelligences" became synonymous with the notion of "learning styles," even though Gardner himself has asserted that there's no evidence connecting the two concepts.[122]

In the early 1990s, Neil Fleming, a school inspector monitoring 9,000 different classes, noticed that there was a lot of variation in how teachers connected with their students. To investigate why some teachers connected to some students and not others, Fleming focused on students' preferences on how information is presented to them.[123] His approach was to ask the students multiple-choice questions about learning. For example:

When I am learning I …

a) like to talk things through.

b) see patterns in things.

c) use examples and applications.

d) read books, articles, and handouts.

Sixteen multiple choice questions, including the one above, comprise the "VARK Questionnaire" that Fleming designed to determine an individual's learning style. By its design, VARK, which stands for Visual, Aural, Read/write, and Kinesthetic, categorizes students by their learning preference, whether by seeing, listening, reading, or physical experience.[124]

Revealing the Data

Evidence to support learning styles is virtually non-existent despite voluminous attempts to validate them. Researchers made the first systematic review of learning styles in 2004 and published their findings in the *Journal of Research in Educational Psychology*. Their evaluation of 71 instruments for determining learning style preferences, like the VARK questionnaire, indicated that more than half of the instruments lacked internal consistency and predictive validity, and 31 percent had no test-retest reliability. The researchers' conclusion was not to base any student learning solely on any learning style instruments.[125]

In 2008, researchers conducted an extensive literature review to evaluate whether there was any evidence supporting the claim that personalized instruction based on learning styles had any effect on learning outcomes. The researchers found virtually no scientific evidence to validate the educational applications of learning styles. Moreover, very few studies used an experimental methodology that could validate applying learning style approaches to education. Furthermore, of those that did use an appropriate method, several found results that contradict the hypothesis.[126]

Another report published in the *British Journal of Psychology* in 2017 found that students who preferred learning visually thought they would remember pictures better. Those who preferred learning verbally thought they would remember words better. But those preferences did not correlate with what they actually remembered. Essentially, what "learning style" meant, in this case, was that the subjects *liked* words or pictures better, not that words or pictures improved their learning.[127]

More recently, 426 anatomy students took the VARK questionnaire and a study strategies survey to determine whether the students' learning styles and study strategies were correlated and whether either of these affected course outcomes. According to the research, the students' performance in the anatomy class did not correlate with their VARK learning style. There was also no link between the study strategies students reported using and their learning styles. In fact, the study found that only a few specific study strategies, such as the use of the virtual microscope, were more likely to improve the students' performance in the course.[128] In other words, students benefited from the same learning strategies and approaches, regardless of their learning styles as reported by their VARK results.

Making an Effort

The myth that some people can learn only in certain ways perpetuates a mindset—in schools, academia, and corporate offices—that gives people an excuse not to learn. This narrow thinking causes some to dismiss learning opportunities throughout their lives and ignore the undeniable truth that learning is uncomfortable. In fact, those students who receive learning catered to their style may be at a disadvantage because they miss out on opportunities to strengthen necessary skills like visual/verbal skills. [129]

Our human brains all learn in similar ways. Preferences are just that, preferences. Unfortunately, there's no evidence to show that such preferences improve our ability to learn. The simple truth is that *leaning in* to the discomfort of learning is a necessary part of the process of learning.

Before becoming a professor of psychology at the University of Pennsylvania, Angela Duckworth, author of *Grit: The Power of Passion and Perseverance,* was an elementary school math and science teacher. She found through her work that the secret to achievement is not talent but a unique blend of passion and persistence she calls "grit." In her experience, what really drives success is not "genius" but a unique combination of desire and long-term perseverance. [130]

Some have framed Duckworth's research and assertions of grit as anti-IQ, but she makes clear that talent exists yet argues that our focus on talent is distracting us from something that is just as important: making an effort. [131] So, if we look at the first two myths and the lessons learned in debunking these falsehoods, we can understand that learning requires two foundational elements: a belief in one's abilities to learn and making an effort to learn.

Myth #3: The same learning strategies that got us here will get us there.

In my line of work, I've noticed that people often view the way they've learned something as the best way to learn anything. A few years ago, at the height of his career, a middle-aged business leader told me a story about how he learned something at the beginning of his career, 25 years prior. He was passionate about using that approach to train new hires at his company. Similarly, I have been in classes where teachers have been teaching using the same strategies for 10, 20, or even 30 years.

You might recall from Chapter 3 that we have learned more about how we learn and how the brain works in the last 20 years than in the 200 years prior. What is problematic with the "what-worked-in-the-past" approach is the underlying assumption that our understanding of teaching and learning has not evolved or doesn't need to improve.

Consider a medical analogy. If you went to the doctor with a bad knee and your doctor recommended the same treatment in 2020 as he had suggested in 1995, you probably would want a second opinion. Suppose your knee requires surgery—it would be unimaginable to use an outdated surgical technique in the operating room. Advances in medical science have enabled more effective, less invasive methods to restore the functioning of the knee. We don't accept outdated approaches to medicine. But many of us will accept outdated approaches to learning with the belief that the same learning strategies that worked in the past remain the best option.

Though there are many examples where psychology and neuroscience have revealed better methods and tools for learning, we continue to leverage widely outdated techniques. We have only scratched the surface on uncovering new strategies, and their adoption has been painfully slow because of this stubborn myth that the same learning strategies that got us here will carry us into the future.

Consider another example: sports. My daughter plays volleyball, and her coaches often use a technique called "blocked practice" to help players develop their serve (a very important component in the game, if you aren't familiar). In blocked practice, the players repeat the same skill over and over before progressing on to another skill, like setting. Here's an example of a "blocked" drill I found online, appropriately termed "Target Aim:"

> "Place a ball cart in any zone on the court, preferably the two back corners on the opposite side of the net. Line up the entire team with balls behind the end line. Allow the players to serve one at a time. The object is to directly hit the ball cart target to earn three points. A missed hit earns zero. The first player to reach fifteen points gets to sit while the rest of the team completes laps or sprints. Teaching players to hit targets on the court gives them an extremely valuable skill."[132]

Yet, what does science tell us about learning a new skill? Cognitive psychologists Dominic Simon and Robert Bjork designed a study that compared this blocked practice method to randomized practice using a keyboarding exercise. They found that participants who practiced a particular keyboarding drill using block practice seemed to do better during the practice session. However, those that used more randomized learning approaches showed greater retention for what was learned and *performed better in the long term*. What's more, those that used blocked practice were more likely to suffer from the "metacognitive illusion" that their skill was better than it actually was.[133]

Despite this advance in understanding learning, demonstrated by this and other studies, many coaches, music teachers, language teachers, and other skills instructors continue to drill using blocked practice.

In the volleyball example, an alternative approach to learning to serve would be more random or intermittent serving, that is, to practice serving while developing other skills needed in volleyball, such as passing, setting, blocking, and digging. Even better would be introducing random disturbances or variations, such as someone yelling while the player is serving or someone from the opposing team running back and forth. In other words, the best approach might not be unlike playing an actual game.

In Chapter 3, I discussed the origins of our ideas about learning and how the evolution of those theories over generations has deepened our understanding of ourselves and how we learn. Significant headway has been made in the last 50 years alone.

Suppose we're to take advantage of the new strategies and methods that are destined to uncap our potential and make us resilient in the face of accelerated change. In that case, we need to focus our attention and efforts on the scientific approach to learning. We must be open to new ways of learning.

Myth #4: We Stop Learning as Adults.

Perhaps one of the most well-known images is the "The Great Wave off Kanagawa" by Katsushika Hokusai, one of the most popular and imitated artists of all time. His paintings and woodblock prints profoundly influenced the development of the 19th-century European painters Van Gogh, Monet, and Degas, and "The Great Wave" remains today the quintessential image of Japanese art.[134]

4.2 The Great Wave off Kanagawa, Katsushika Hokusai (c. 1828-1833): Adorning the walls of museums, Pinterest boards, and frat houses alike, the classic painting is ubiquitous and uncontroversial in its beauty.

What many do not know is that Hokusai was in his 70s when he created that famous print. The artist saw himself as a continual learner of art throughout his life and never considered ending the expansion of his knowledge and skill. Hokusai wrote:

> *"Ever since I was six, I have been obsessed with drawing the shapes of things. By the time I was fifty, I had published countless drawings, but nothing I produced before the age of seventy is worthy of note. Not until I was seventy-three, did I begin to understand the structure of nature as it truly is, the structure of animals, plants, trees, birds, fish and insects. Thus, by the time I am eighty, I will have made some real progress. At ninety I will have fathomed the mystery of things; at a hundred I will surely have reached a phenomenal level, and when I'm a hundred and ten, everything I do, be it a dot or a line, will be alive."* [135]

Stories of people learning throughout their lives are not rare or difficult to find. You see examples of it in every field of interest. American cooking expert, author, and television personality Julia Child (1912-2004) studied history in college and began a career with the CIA as a research assistant, which enabled her to travel. On one of her overseas assignments, she met her husband, Paul Child, who also worked in Intelligence in present-day Sri Lanka. When they moved back to the United States, Julia enrolled in a cooking school to prepare for married life (this was the mid-1940s) and found she wasn't a very good cook. Paul was quoted at the time as saying, *"I was willing to put up with that awful cooking to get Julia."*[136]

The couple moved to Paris, and Julia's first French meal impressed her so much that she enrolled in Le Cordon Bleu's famed Parisian cooking school, a year later at the age of 37. She published her first book, *Mastering the Art of French Cooking, Volume One*, in 1961 at the age of 49.[137]

Julia Child introduced French cuisine to Americans and became one of the world's all-time favorite chefs and beloved television personalities, inspiring millions of people to learn to cook with her cheerful voice and passion for cooking. She once famously said, *"No one is born a great cook; one learns by doing."*[138]

There are likely millions of examples of people finding success later in life. Yet the idea that "it's too late to learn" still permeates our culture and creates the mindset that we become less adept at learning as we grow older and develop the sense that we are "done learning."

While aging does affect the brain, particularly when it comes to processing speed, modern psychology and advances in neuroscience and genetics have shed new light on a critical fact: **there is no endpoint to learning**. As I will share in more detail in the next chapter, neuroscientists report that the brain continues to form new neural pathways even into late adulthood. This hardwired ability in each of us is called neuroplasticity. Research also shows that older brains are better at complex problem-solving and information synthesis than younger brains.[139]

The myth that we stop learning at a point in our lives needlessly truncates human potential—at a time when HI is needed more than ever. The truth is, when people believe they've stopped learning or can no longer learn, it limits their capability to learn because they no longer put deliberate and intentional effort into learning. But learning, as you will see later in this book, is something we are all capable of doing, well into our 90s. And the power of intention alone increases our capacity to learn.

Our Beliefs Matter

The underlying theme in this chapter is that the four myths of learning perpetuate attitudes that constrain our collective and individual ability to learn. Belief in these myths shapes our reality, and, therefore, influences our behavior. It's time to reword these myths into new, more scientifically based views:

Intelligence—and who we are—is not fixed. Everyone can learn. We should inspire and support everyone's learning to the height of their capacity. Studies show that when people are encouraged to view intelligence as malleable, they're more engaged with learning.

We all learn through effort. Learning requires two foundational elements: a belief in one's abilities to learn; and trying to learn. Instruction should not be based on any singular learning style; preferences certainly come into play but leaning into the discomfort of learning is a necessary part of learning.

The same learning strategies that got us here won't get us there. We are learning new ways to learn that have the potential to elevate our capabilities and make us resilient in the face of accelerated change. We need to constantly re-evaluate and improve how we learn if we are to adapt.

We continue learning as adults. The science is irrefutable. Modern psychology and advances in neuroscience and genetics have shed new light on a critical fact: there is no endpoint to learning. We are capable of learning throughout our lives.

The next chapter on the neuroscience of learning presents a tipping point in our beliefs about learning. Quite possibly, for the first time in the history of learning and education, modern neuroscience is dispelling myths about learning, relegating them to artifacts of what someday may be viewed as the dark ages of our understanding about learning. We are experiencing a nascent renaissance in learning, potentially unleashing human capability beyond limits previously imagined.

5

The Limitless Human Potential to Learn

"Human beings are works in progress that mistakenly think they're finished."

—Dan Gilbert

Occasionally, I will talk to a young adult who holds onto the belief that the person they are now is the same person they will be for the rest of their lives. That is not unusual: most people tend to overestimate the staying power of their values and beliefs, or even in their preferences in such things as music, sports, or hobbies, and underestimate their capacity to continue to learn and grow.

Harvard social psychologist Daniel Gilbert calls this the "End-of-History Illusion"—that the person we are today is the person who we were always meant to be."[140] Dr. Gilbert and his colleagues coined this term in a 2013 study measuring the personalities, values, and preferences of more than 19,000 people 18 to 68 years of age. Participants were asked how much they had changed in the past ten years and to predict how much they would change in the next ten years.[141]

Individuals of all ages reported that they have experienced significant personal growth and changes up to the present moment but believe that they will not substantially grow or mature beyond that in the future. The study indicates that people tend to regard their current state of being as a concluded moment when they have become fully the person they will be for the rest of their lives. The study also reveals that people tend to underpredict how much their preferences, values, and even personalities change over time.[142]

Still, when you stop and reflect on yourself twenty, ten, or even five years ago, you might notice how profoundly you have changed. Experiences, events, and circumstances shape our life trajectories in unique ways. And simply growing older can shape our perspectives. Consider your favorite movie, song, hobby, or car ten years ago. Perhaps you are better at managing your emotions or showing compassion and empathy. Perhaps, like Julia Child, you have learned to cook.

The End of History Illusion: When we are younger, we think we will always carry certain traits with us, such as our favorite song or our disdain for tomatoes. While we certainly adjust to this reality with age, we generally don't acknowledge or predict the magnitude of future change.

The concept of seeing ourselves as the fully realized version of who we are causes myopia of sorts that permeates much of our thinking. Consider how you view others and whether you see people as who they are right now or who they were years ago. So much potential for growth and knowing is unleashed when we see ourselves on a journey of continual development. And the primary facilitator of this gradual unfolding is our brain, which, as you will discover, is constantly learning and remodeling itself based on our experiences, our view of the world, and our view of ourselves within it.

Stem Cells in the Adult Brain

After decades of studying neurons, specialized brain cells designed to transmit information to other nerve cells, muscles, or glands, Nobel Prize winner Santiago Ramón y Cajal (1852-1934), the father of modern neuroscience, wrote what would become a decades-long cannon: adult brains do not grow:

> *"Once the development was ended, the founts of growth and regeneration of the axons and dendrites dried up irrevocably. In the adult centers, the nerve paths are something fixed, ended, and immutable. Everything may die, nothing may be regenerated. It is for the science of the future to change, if possible, this harsh decree."*[143]

Cajal's assertion that the formation of new brain cells stopped once people reached adulthood was taught to generations of medical students and biologists. However, over the last two decades, mounting evidence has confirmed that the brain forms new neural pathways and creates new brain cells in adulthood and well into old age.

Neural stem cells (NSCs) were first discovered in the 1960s, and our knowledge about these blood cells produced by bone marrow has continued to grow ever since. By the early 1990s and the advent of structural and functional magnetic resonance imaging technology (MRI and fMRI), neurogenesis (the growth of brain cells) in the adult brain could no longer be disputed.[144] Today, it is generally accepted that the adult brain is far from being fixed in its growth.

We humans have a limitless potential to learn, and we appear to be evolving to be more intelligent as time goes on. Studies show that our IQ as a species has been rising steadily. A 2015 study published in the journal *Intelligence* presented the results of a sixty-year longitudinal study by psychologists who set out to determine the status of "world IQ." Researchers collecting the IQ scores of over 200,000 people from 48 different countries found that global IQ has risen 20 points since 1950.[145]

One reason for this improvement is the "Flynn Effect," named after researcher James R. Flynn, who attributed the increase in IQ scores to improvements in education and better nutrition. Flynn also surmises that we have gotten better at test-taking and critically thinking in the abstract, which is what an IQ test assesses.[146] In addition to improving our increased proficiency at taking tests, we have also amassed more collective knowledge than ever before. Our ability to integrate and apply that knowledge has been increasing over time, aided by advances in digitalization.

Neurons and Synapses

What is most remarkable about the human brain and how it functions is the unique way our brain cells—stimulated by thoughts, emotions, and physical activity—transmit information to each other to ultimately direct and support our actions and reactions to the world around us.

We are truly gifted with a uniquely sizeable biological capability to process information. The number of neurons and synapses occurring in the human brain is unparalleled in nature. The human brain's learning infrastructure is made up of an estimated 86 billion neurons linked to one another via hundreds of trillions of tiny contact points called synapses.[147] Each neuron consists of a large cell body and nucleus with a very thin strand called an axon that transmits cell information. Dendrites receive and process that information.

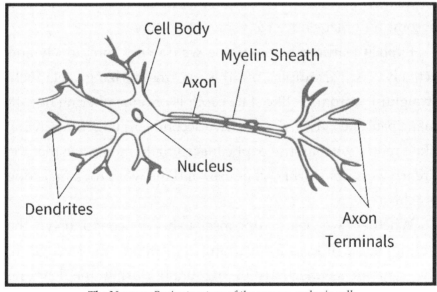

The Neuron: Basic structure of the neuron, or brain cell.

Neurons run on electricity. As an electrical signal passes down its axon, the axon tip releases chemicals called neurotransmitters, and a synapse or connection occurs as nerve impulses pass from one neuron to another. These neurotransmitters direct the dendrites of the receiving neuron to absorb the information and activate its own electrical charge, and if informed to do so, send an electrical signal to the next neuron in the chain.[148]

How Learning Happens

We don't have a single system for learning but rather have multiple systems for different kinds of information. The two primary types of learning are implicit and explicit. Implicit learning occurs when we do not have conscious awareness of what we are learning.[149] An example of this is early language acquisition or riding a bike. Implicit memories are skills that become automatic once we've mastered them.

Explicit learning is something we do very consciously and actively. An example of this is memorizing relatively straightforward facts like state capitols or remembering how to make pancakes. Also, if we learn a second language later in life, like French, we may use explicit learning to memorize that the French word for shirt is "chemise" and the word for a male dog is "chien."

Whether we learn unconsciously or consciously, the physiological process for learning is related to the strength of the synaptic connections in the brain during the learning process. The term "Hebbian learning" comes from the work of Donald Hebb (1904-1985), a Canadian psychologist who proposed a neurophysiological explanation for learning and memory based on a simple principle:

"When an axon of cell A is near enough to excite a cell B and repeatedly or persistently takes part in firing it, some growth process or metabolic change takes place in one or both cells such that A's efficiency, as one of the cells firing B, is increased."[150]

Hebb's principle was coined into a rhyme that has since become a popular saying in neuroscience—*"what fires together, wires together"*—meaning the more you exercise a neural circuit in your brain, the stronger that circuit becomes.[151] For instance, the more you practice a musical instrument, or speak a different language, or play a sport, or draw portraits, the more fluid and skilled you become.

Hebb proposed that when two neurons fire together, sending off impulses simultaneously, the connections between them—the synapses—grow stronger. When this happens, learning has taken place.[152]

Learning from a Snail

To better understand how learning depends on the strength of synaptic connections, we can look at the work of Nobel Laureate and Columbia University professor and scientist Dr. Eric Kandel (1929-) who has studied biological mechanisms underlying learning and memory at a fundamental cellular and molecular level.[153]

To study learning and memory, Kandel and his team took a reductionist approach and searched for an animal in which a simple behavior could be modified, and vital connections between its neural system and environment could be isolated.

According to Kandel, as he explained in his Nobel lecture, there are no fundamental differences between the neurons and synapses of humans and those of a snail. Kandel chose the sea slug *Aplysia Californica* for its simple neural system with uniquely identifiable nerve cells. Aplysia has only 20,000 nerve cells, whereas the mammalian brain has a million million central nerve cells.[154]

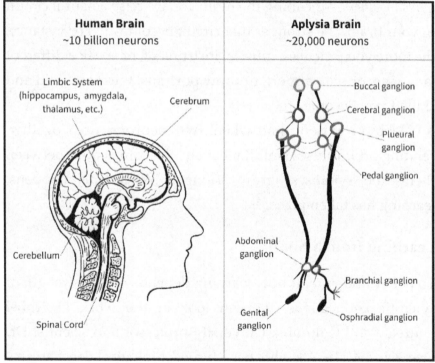

Human Brain and Aplysia Brain: Aplysia neurons are the largest in the animal kingdom, and they have comparatively few, making them an excellent subject for experimental research.

While working with this less complex neural system, Kandel and his team were able to study the sea slug's gill and siphon withdrawal reflex, a defensive response when the animal is disturbed, such as through touch to the snail's siphon.

The researchers found that the synaptic connection responsible for this simple reflex could either be weakened or strengthened through learning.[155] For example, though touch to the animal's siphon results in gill-withdrawal, after repeated touch, the response would weaken. Essentially, the snail, having learned that the touch is harmless, stops withdrawing its gill. This behavior change, *habituation*, is the same type of behavior change that occurs when we learn to "block out" certain noises after repeated or lengthy exposure.[156]

Kandel and his team were able to observe evidence of Hebbian learning theory: habituation leads to a weakening of synaptic connections between the sensory neurons that detect the stimulus and the motor neurons that react. Similarly, sensitization, performed through administering an aversive shock before touching the siphon, leads to strengthening of the same connections as well as increased excitability of the neurons. What's more, the team found that these changes persist, indicating that synaptic connections do indeed store both short- and long-term memories.[157] Neurons that fire together do certainly wire together, as Hebb had proposed.

While we still have a lot to learn about the different ways we learn, we do know implicit and explicit learning involves different parts of the brain. In explicit learning, strengthening a synapse cannot create a learning experience or memory on its own. Changes and connections made and strengthened throughout the brain are necessary to create a thorough memory.

For example, suppose you are trying to memorize how to drive to work. Explicit memory — or memory for people, places, and objects—requires information from several senses. The hippocampus integrates this information and creates a cognitive map of the external environment.

Memory Central

The most important part of the brain responsible for memory is the hippocampus, located in one of the oldest regions of the brain, the limbic system. The hippocampus is a small, seahorse-shaped section that is crucial for long-term memory formation and spatial navigation. Without it, you would not be able to recall memories or form new memories, such as what day it is or the names of the people on your team at work. Nor would you be able to form associations among people, things, and events. More recent studies show that the hippocampus is also responsible for feeding information to brain areas responsible for learning.[158]

Using fMRI scanning, the neuroscience research team at Arizona State University found that the hippocampus encoded associations during learning. These links are used by other brain systems such as the amygdala and cerebellum, which are also responsible for learning.[159] This recognition of brain-wide involvement has led neuroscientists to search for how information is transmitted, processed, and stored in the brain to bring about learning or the formation of a memory.

Researchers are also studying the size and structure of the hippocampus of people and groups with highly developed skills. In one such ten-year-long study, researchers at the University College of London used MRI scans to measure the effect that memorization has on the human brain, specifically, the brains of London taxi drivers.[160]

People say that earning a license to drive one of London's iconic black cabs is equivalent to earning an advanced college degree and that being able to navigate the streets isn't just considered knowledge but is formally called "The Knowledge." While earning their certificates, London taxi drivers-in-training spend three to four years driving around the city on mopeds, memorizing a maze of 25,000 streets as well as thousands of tourist attractions.[161]

The researchers found that London taxi drivers have not only larger-than-average hippocampi, but that their intensive training is responsible for the growth of their memory centers. They found that there is a capability for change in the structure of the healthy adult human brain in response to environmental demands.[162]

In another field, researchers are finding that absolute pitch (AP), the ability of some musicians to accurately identify and name musical tones in isolation, is associated with structural changes in the brain. Even though the neural mechanisms enabling this capability are still unclear, researchers find that musicians have thicker regions of the auditory cortex than non-musicians.[163]

At first, it was assumed that these cortex differences were present at birth and must have prompted those individuals to pursue music as a career, then excel at it because of their thicker auditory structures. But brain imaging now reveals that the structure of the brain changes through learning and practice and that physical changes in the brain can happen much faster during learning than might be expected.[164]

For example, through imaging, neuroscientists at the University of Lausanne in Switzerland witnessed increases in the volume of gray matter in medical students' brains after they studied for an examination. Additionally, researchers at Tel Aviv University showed that 16 laps around a racetrack in a computerized video game were enough to cause changes in a new player's hippocampal brain region, that area of the brain critical for spatial learning and navigation.[165]

Neuroplasticity

Neuroplasticity, the brain's ability to change and adapt both structurally and functionally in response to life experiences,[166] has become a popular catchword. Neuroscientists once believed that this plasticity only occurred early in life, but we now know that our brain cells have plasticity or malleability throughout our lives. Neuroplasticity, however, does tend to diminish with age because as we learn, we strengthen some connections while weakening others through pruning. This forges a sort of regulation network for new information.

The first use of the term "plasticity" is credited to three neuroscientists: Eugenio Tanzi for first identifying connections between neurons as possible sites of neural plasticity; Ernesto Lugaro for first measuring how effectively neurons connect to each other; and Santiago Ramón y Cajal with his own hypothesis of plasticity in the formation of new connections between neurons in the cerebral cortex.[167]

The basic idea of neuroplasticity is that brain activity stimulates the brain to reorganize its connections.[168] Brain reorganization takes place by several mechanisms, including:[169]

- axonal sprouting, where axons grow new nerve endings to reconnect neurons

- synapse formation, the strengthening of synapses on the dendrites

- dendritic pruning, the brain's way to maintain efficient brain function through eliminating extra synapses

- neurogenesis, the formation of new neurons

In addition to referring to the brain's ability to change and adapt due to activity, neuroplasticity also refers to the brain's ability to repair itself. For example, neuroplasticity allows the neurons in the brain to compensate for brain injury or disease through the reorganization and creation of new neural pathways.[170] Undamaged axons can sprout nerve endings and connect with other undamaged nerve cells, thus making new links and new neural pathways to restore a damaged function.[171]

Jill Bolte Taylor, an American neuroanatomist and public speaker, suffered a stroke and witnessed first-hand how her brain functions shut down one by one: motion, speech, memory, and self-awareness. She had to relearn how to eat and how to talk. Even in her forties, she was able to reestablish new pathways to accomplish this because of neuroplasticity.[172]

Taylor spent eight years recovering her ability to think, walk, and talk. She has since become a spokesperson for stroke recovery and for the possibility of coming back from brain injury stronger than before. In her case, although the stroke damaged the left side of her brain, her highly active recovery released a flow of creative energy from her right hemisphere.

Neurogenesis

Perhaps one of the most thought-provoking phenomena of neuroplasticity is neurogenesis or the production of new brain cells. After decades of believing that neurogenesis stops when we reach adulthood, we now know that the human brain can generate new neurons throughout an individual's life, particularly in the hippocampus, a part of the brain that continues to grow in humans well into our nineties.[173]

While the mechanisms underlying adult neurogenesis remain unclear, there is increasing evidence that adult-born dentate granule cells (DGCs) make important contributions to learning and memory as they mature and become fully integrated into the brain circuitry.[174]

We now know that the human brain is a highly dynamic and constantly reorganizing cognitive system. It is shaped and reshaped at some level by every experience we have across our entire lifespan. Moreover, by working harder to improve your brain's function and rate of growth, you can redirect and thicken neural pathways and increase your ability to learn. It is possible to develop new neural pathways to reinvent yourself and learn a new skill. You can overcome stressful events and fear-based memories that may be preventing you from applying yourself and extracting the most out of life.

The School Sisters of Notre Dame

In 1986, Dr. David Snowdon, one of the world's leading experts on Alzheimer's disease, initiated a longitudinal study with 678 American Roman Catholic sisters who were members of the School Sisters of Notre Dame in Mankato, Minneapolis, Minnesota. The purpose of what came to be known as the "Nun Study" was to assess the effects of aging and determine whether *"linguistic ability in early life is associated with cognitive function and Alzheimer's disease in late life."* [175]

The participants, ranging in age from 75 to 104, agreed to provide access to their medical and personal histories and written documents; and, after death, to donate their brain tissue to the project. Among the documents submitted were autobiographical essays written by the nuns when they joined the sisterhood in their twenties.

Nuns offered a near-perfect control group for the study, given the similarity in living conditions, health care, and lifestyle (no drug use and very little to no alcohol consumption) that was much harder to control for in other studies. Additionally, none of these women had ever been married or had children.

One of the significant findings from the Nun Study was how the participants' lifestyle, education, higher linguistic ability, and continuous learning may have protected them against Alzheimer's disease and dementia. Additionally, participants who had a bachelor's degree or higher education were less likely to develop Alzheimer's later in life. [176]

Perhaps the most surprising result of the study is the discovery that the way we express ourselves in language, even at an early age, can to a certain degree predict how long we will live and how vulnerable we will be to Alzheimer's as we age. Upon reviewing each of the sister's autobiographic essays written back in their twenties, researchers found that lack of "linguistic density" (complexity, vivacity, fluency) was a significant predictor of its author's risk of developing Alzheimer's disease in old age. The study also found that the nuns who wrote positively (positive sentences, positive words, and positive emotions) in their journals were more likely to live longer than their counterparts.[177]

Snowdon also found that the consumption of certain antioxidants, an optimistic outlook, and exercise were inversely correlated with the development of Alzheimer's disease. Participants who engaged in some daily exercise regimen were more likely to retain cognitive abilities in their later years. Many of the nuns were mentally active throughout their lives, engaging in activities such as learning to play piano and learning new languages well into old age.[178]

There could be other dynamics as well, such as a linked culture of learning and dynamism for learning among all the sisters in the convent. That bodes well for organizations looking to build a culture of learning and resilience.

Resilience and Determination Develop Pathways

We can discover a great deal about the benefits of learning and other behaviors from studying Alzheimer's Disease. One such discovery can come from the remarkable findings from David

Snowdon's Nun Study. It was found that when the sisters died and their brains were donated for autopsy, despite the presence of Alzheimer's in some of the brains examined, the nuns who had belonged to these brains showed no signs of having the disease while they were alive.[179]

According to Lisa Genova, neuroscientist and writer, it is because these nuns had a high level of "cognitive reserve," which is a way of saying that they had more functional synapses. People who have more years of formal education, a high degree of literacy, and regularly engage in mentally stimulating activities all tend to have more cognitive reserve.[180]

Genova postulates that ongoing learning can cause people with Alzheimer's not to show visible cognitive impairment because continuous cognitive activity creates neural pathways that are thickened by habit, practice, and determination to learn.[181]

Two-Lane vs. Six-Lane Highway

The linguistic ability of the School Sisters of Notre Dame, their positive outlook on life, and continuously learning throughout life resulted in their having better cognitive function later in life. Their neural pathways were diverse and fortified, so Alzheimer's Disease was less likely to damage all of one pathway.

Think of brain disease like lane closures on a highway. If there's a lane closure in both directions on a two-lane highway, and there are no alternative routes, traffic will stop, and there will be no way to get around the closure. On the other hand, if there's a lane closure in both directions on a six-lane highway and there are alternative routes, you may not even notice the closure.

Six Lane Highway: *Your brain uses many pathways for the same reason Los Angeles has six lanes on the 405—because it needs to.*

The past 25 years of neuroscience have not only illuminated incorrect thinking about the brain, but it's also revealing that despite how much we know, we still know very little about the underlying mechanisms of the brain's ability to learn and its resilience in the face of injury and disease. Increasingly, we are discovering evidence that our brains, at any age, are endlessly capable of growth and adaptation and that we can positively affect this capability through our own actions. The subsequent chapters continue to build on this theme and will empower you to live into your undeniable and inexhaustible ability to grow.

Part 3

Strategies for Learning

6

The Barriers to Learning

"To know that you are a prisoner of your mind is the dawn of wisdom."

—Nisargadatta Maharaj

When I reflect on all the things that hold us back from our potential to learn, I notice that they all have one thing in common: our mindset. Recall from Chapter 3 the subject of cognitive psychology and the concept of schemata, our cognitive structures that represent our general knowledge about things, and how those mental maps help us learn or assimilate new knowledge.

Paradoxically, our mental maps also get in the way of our ability to learn new things. We talked about the 86 billion neurons and hundreds of trillions of synapses in our brain. Still, there are also 100 million sensory receptors in our bodies and 10 trillion synapses firing throughout our central nervous system.[182] This vast array of sensory input demonstrates that our cognitive physiology is incredibly sensitive and continuously reactive to our external environment.

Yet, it is through an intimately personal lens that we assimilate all our knowledge and conceive ideas. Author and therapist Anodea Judith calls our individualized schemata a *personal matrix* of information within our mind.[183] We spend our entire lives incorporating what we learn from our families, friends, schools, workplaces, places of worship, and other influences such as popular culture, politics, and the media. The resulting unique, *personal matrix* we construct in our own minds can delay, or prevent altogether, our ability to learn.

Think of it as a sort of information filtration system. You might recall from Chapter 5 the strengthening of synapses that occurs when we learn, but also remember the pruning of dendrites that weaken, delay, or prevent the growth of other possible neural pathways. I think of it as adaptive neural hygiene. The result is that these morphological changes in our brain enable us to think faster and make decisions.

Our personal matrices undergo constant consolidation and reorganization, and sometimes all it takes is a nudge to disrupt the unique constructions in our minds. Recall the study shared in Chapter 4, where students were encouraged to view intelligence as malleable. They were confident in shifting their fixed mindsets from *"I cannot"* to *"I can"* and obtained higher grade point averages than the two control groups that were not similarly inspired. Awareness of the barriers to learning can help us shift our mindset and open our minds to new opportunities to learn.

I distinguish *Six Barriers to Learning* that affect each of us at one time or another in our lives:

1. Lack of motivation

2. Free riding

3. Ignoring failure

4. Cognitive bias

5. Expertise

6. Moral convictions

You might notice that none of these barriers have anything to do with cognitive ability. Indeed, some people have learning disabilities, but the barriers I define in this chapter are things we can ultimately control, albeit with intent and effort, and not impediments caused by genetic or neurobiological factors.

Lack of Motivation

There are three related needs inherent to learning that when absent can inhibit motivation to learn: 1) *Self-Efficacy*, the confidence you have about your capabilities and that what you do matters; 2) *Intrinsic Motivation*, intrinsic/cultural values around learning; and 3) *Expected Value*, or the return we expect on our investment in learning.

Self-Efficacy

Many beliefs, such as the belief that intelligence is fixed, are deep-rooted in our social and educational systems and negatively affect the motivation to learn.

The concept of self-efficacy was first proposed by Albert Bandura (1925-2021), a Canadian-American psychologist, who in 1977, was searching for a unifying theory of behavior change. Bandura advanced the notion that one's own expectations of their personal efficacy, or ability, determines whether they will initiate coping behaviors—the effort they will expend and how long they will endure in the face of obstacles and aversive experiences.[184] Bandura's theory was that one's sense of self-worth and ability is derived from personal accomplishments, experiences, and encouragements from others. It is also derived from one's physiological state, which includes body and mind, a topic I will delve into later in Chapter 9.

Often described as task-specific self-confidence, educational researchers from diverse fields of study have used the notion of self-efficacy to predict and explain a wide range of human performance, from athletic skill to academic achievement.[185]

Self-efficacy is your certainty in your ability to achieve a goal and the belief that what you do and think matters. It speaks to your trust in your capacity to execute and attain specific performance—from test and term paper grades to production and sales goals. If your self-efficacy is low, your tendency will be to not try. Alternately, if your sense of self-worth is high and you have confidence in your abilities, you will continue to work with conviction and focus on achieving and surpassing your goals.

Carol Dweck's research on fixed mindsets versus growth mindsets builds on this concept of personal efficacy.[186] A person with a fixed mindset, whether they are a teenager studying for a physics exam or a fifty-year-old learning a new skill, would tend to believe that no matter how hard they try, the odds are stacked against them. Those same people with growth mindsets would view the challenges they face as opportunities to learn and grow.

Sometimes this lack of motivation to learn is strongly influenced by social biases, often subconscious, about which groups or individuals do or do not have the cognitive or physical ability to perform. Research shows that people, especially young people, tend to internalize and live out the limitations imposed on them by others' biases.

Dr. Jeffrey Howard, a Harvard-trained psychologist and founder of the Efficacy Institute, has devoted his career to studying the psychological variables that drive performance and how negative expectations from significant others become internalized.[187] His research shows how the negative expectations and messages of doubt and exclusion of minority children by teachers, managers, mentors, and other important figures can have a negative and lasting impact on their self-esteem, leading to a lack of effort and even feelings of helplessness.[188] This, Dr. Howard says, can affect whole groups which may then internalize these messages of doubt and exclusion. *"Once you convey to children—whether consciously or not—that they are too 'dumb' to learn, they will almost always prove you right."*[189]

Intrinsic Motivation

Many of us spend time learning solely for the inherent enjoyment or contentment. In other words, we are intrinsically motivated to learn. Most likely, those of you reading this book are intrinsically motivated to learn. If you have gone to college or trade school or taken a class to advance your career, it is likely you were driven by some combination of intrinsic and extrinsic motivation.

Optimistically, you saw education as a means to advance your success and financial prospects (extrinsic motivation).

Still, you chose what classes you took based on deriving some deep-rooted value from your education (intrinsic motivation), such as interest in the subject, expanding one's knowledge base, or even the enjoyment of engaging in learning activities with classmates.

To what extent are we motivated by extrinsic factors? Philosophers and psychologists throughout the 20th century have explained motivation in terms of instincts (the Freudian approach) or as a result of conditioning (the behaviorist approach). Since the 1950s, behaviorists commanded the study of motivation, producing volumes of research showing how offering extrinsic rewards and incentives (such as money or good grades) could condition human drive and motives over time.[190]

In 1984, University of Rochester psychologists Richard Ryan and Edward Deci published the culmination of years of research, *Intrinsic Motivation and Self-Determination in Human Behavior.* In this seminal work, the authors advanced the concept of Self-Determination Theory, which sharply contrasts long-standing beliefs about human motivation.[191]

In the broadest sense, the theory, as it has developed over the past quarter-century, maintains that motivation develops from within us. It is grounded in our basic psychological needs to develop our skills and capacities, to act of our own accord, and to connect to others and our environment. Deci and Ryan refer to these needs as "competency, autonomy, and relatedness."[192] According to self-determination theory, we are most deeply engaged and do our most creative work when we feel that we are acting according to our own will on behalf of goals we find meaningful.

Deci and Ryan's most surprising discovery was that rewards, such as prizes and money, were not only less effective than behavioral psychologists had long supposed, but under some circumstances, could *diminish* people's feelings of engagement and motivation.[193]

In their famous Soma cube study, Deci divided college students into two groups and placed each group in a room with a Soma cube puzzle game and an assortment of magazines. He instructed the participants to work on the Soma cube puzzle but offered to pay the members of one group for each design they correctly assembled. After some time, Deci told the students that puzzle-solving time was over, adding that he would leave for about 10 minutes to record data and return with a questionnaire.

But rather than record data, he observed the groups from outside the rooms. He saw a noticeable difference: to a significant degree, paid participants were more likely to put down the puzzles and pick up the magazines. Participants who weren't paid, on the other hand, were more likely to continue working on the puzzles.

In clarifying their findings further, Deci and Ryan noticed that ex-post-facto recognition of outstanding work improved motivation. Their work demonstrates a distinction between the effects of rewards offered as incentives, which tended to dampen motivation, and those presented as recognition of exemplary work, which often enhanced motivation.[194]

In the years since, other researchers have produced hundreds of studies that show variations on that theme.[195] Studies showing grade-schoolers who weren't told they were being tested performing better on assessments than the students who were informed. There are also studies showing that kids permitted a range of choices were better at regulating their emotions and behavior over time than kids raised in authoritarian environments. And studies of adults show a correlation between job autonomy and the ability to respond creatively to challenges.

Perceived Value

As people get older, they sometimes lose their motivation to learn new things. And even though all the recent neurological research disproves the myth that we stop learning as adults, we tend to evaluate the perceived value—the cost and reward—that comes with a particular action such as learning something new. Ann Graybiel, an Institute Professor at MIT and Investigator at the McGovern Institute for Brain Research, adds that *"As we age, we find it harder to have a get-up-and-go attitude toward things."*[196]

MIT neuroscientists have now identified in mice a brain circuit that is critical for maintaining this kind of motivation.[197] This circuitry is particularly important for learning to make decisions that require evaluating the cost-benefit that comes with a particular action. The researchers showed that they could boost older mice's motivation to engage in this type of learning by reactivating cell structures associated with habit formation, control of voluntary movement, emotion, and addiction.[198]

The researchers also found that these structures play a significant role in a type of decision-making known as approach-avoidance conflict.[199] These decisions involve choosing whether to take the good with the bad or avoid both when given options that have both positive and negative consequences. Examples of these types of decisions include accepting a job offer that pays more but requires a move to another city and away from family and friends, taking a pay cut or losing your job, or starting a family versus pursuing a career. As we get older, we are more likely to avoid these decisions altogether so as not to provoke the uncomfortable feeling of having to decide.

But there is probably something else at play here. Recent studies show that adults have to work harder on cognitive tasks than their more youthful peers. While somewhat speculative, neuroimaging shows that older adults muster more brain functions to solve cognitive problems and need more environmental support to engage in some kinds of cognitive learning activities.[200] Together, these two findings may indicate that the cost of learning increases as we get older while the perceived benefit declines.

Free Riding

Remora, also known as suckerfish, is a species of marine fish noted for attaching themselves and riding about on large marine animals and even ocean-going vessels. This allows the remora to travel to different areas without having to apply any of its own energy to swim.

In economic terms, the remora fish are the principal actors in the *Free Rider Problem*. This term was initially used in the mid-19th century to describe people who rode the trains without paying for a seat. In economics, the term is chiefly used to describe a situation where individuals or groups obtain benefits from a resource or good without paying for that use.[201]

A simple example might be in benefiting from another person's work without payment or exchange. If your partner or roommate always cleans the kitchen, you receive the benefits of a clean kitchen without having to contribute anything yourself. You are a free rider. Micro examples of the free-rider problem appear everywhere, such as waiting for a friend to pick a restaurant and make the reservation or letting your friend devise the travel route. As another example, consider if your friend constantly borrows your lawnmower without ever offering to pay for the upkeep or fill the gas tank.

We can see free riding in the workplace as well. When new technologies emerge, many people will wait for others to learn the technologies and use them first. A middle-aged woman recently told me that she asked her son to learn how to perform certain functions on her new smartphone and then show her how to do it. There are people who put in the extra effort and invest the extra time to learn, while others ride for free.

Being a free rider is okay some of the time. There are always going to be situations where there is one person less tolerant of a dirty kitchen or someone who's savvy enough to learn and adopt technology early and share it with others.

The problem with free riders is that free-riding results in what economists call a *market failure* because individual incentives are not aligned with optimal outcomes for all. A free rider benefits from the good without having to pay for it while others bear the cost. In many cases, the free-rider problem involves a public good, such as clean air or national defense, both of which everyone can benefit from even if only some individuals are contributing effort or taxes and others are not.

Free riding is a natural by-product of our social nature, but when it comes to learning, some are *habitual free riders*. The result is that, collectively, the group loses from everyone not learning and sharing what they are learning. Individually, the habitual free rider loses because they are not doing the hard work of figuring things out for themselves. Learning is a skill, and those not regularly practicing learning are reducing their ability to grow their brains and leaving future potential on the table.

If you look at the benefits gained from human learning, it is, in essence, a public good. Consider the Covid vaccine or any number of technological advances as an example. If too many of us are free riding, we are missing out on collective human potential. Given we are at a point where Human Intelligence (HI) is needed more than ever, increased awareness of free riding is critical.

Ignoring Failure

Failure is one of the greatest teachers, but failure lessons are often hidden in plain sight. I recently met someone who had started recording a regular podcast. He had produced dozens of episodes but hadn't been able to get more than a handful of listeners. The most recent podcast had as many listeners as the first, no doubt friends and family. When I asked him about what he had learned thus far and what changes he has made since the inception, he responded in a way that demonstrated he didn't understand that I was prodding for lessons learned and how he responded to them.

No doubt you have been in similar situations yourself: a fitness regimen or diet that isn't working, trouble staying within a budget, a problem at work that seems to follow someone wherever they go. Dubbed "the ostrich effect"[202] by University of Sheffield psychologist Thomas Webb and his colleagues, the problem of avoiding negative information causes many to "bury their head in the sand" when it comes to measuring goal progress.

In addition to wanting to avoid negative information, people often do not realize failures contain useful information. Across five studies involving 11 separate samples (N = 1238), people were reluctant to share stories about failure with others, particularly when it came to professional experiences.[203] In the studies, participants were far more likely to share stories of successes, even when they ostensibly provided very little learning opportunity.[204] The study demonstrates that failure, while common, is often hidden.

When we ignore our failures, without examining them, we miss the important work of identifying themes and defining principles that can guide us, our work, our leadership, and our relationships. We create a barrier to learning when we fail to see, share, and learn from failure.

The Sunk Cost Fallacy

Perhaps a perfect example of covering up a mistake is rationalizing a costly decision by investing more in that bad decision. What typifies this barrier to learning is our bias to follow through on a sub-optimal undertaking because we have already invested money, time, and effort.

One of my favorite examples of sunk cost is from a study of car usage in Singapore, a small, densely populated island in Asia that is constantly burdened by significant traffic congestion. Since 1975, the Singapore government has attempted to mitigate car usage through tolls and by limiting the number of vehicles allowed on the streets, especially in the most congested areas.[205]

A result of the government's policy to limit car ownership is that retail prices of cars in Singapore are the world's highest.[206] In terms of sunk cost, a study on car usage in Singapore shows that people use their cars (versus other forms of transportation) much more frequently if the vehicle is costly versus inexpensive. Moreover, Singaporeans feel compelled to drive more rather than less to justify the high price tags for their cars.[207]

In essence, automobile owners are doubling down on a costly initial decision by paying more for gas and toll charges when it would be less expensive to minimize driving altogether. Instead, Singaporean drivers mistakenly view their car as a cost that can be recouped and frame their thinking around the mindset of *"getting my money's worth."*

There are many examples of the sunk cost mentality surfacing as a barrier to learning in our personal life, in the business world, and government. It often expresses itself as, *"I have a lot vested in this."* We will watch a bad movie through to the end because we paid for it, even though watching it means wasting even more valuable time. In organizational settings, we will even patch a flawed process that has been limping along for years when we might get a better result from starting over. Because of the sunk cost fallacies that shroud our better choices and decisions, we will often double-down on our own failures instead of moving forward and learning from mistakes.

Cognitive Bias

Our brains constantly scan for patterns in the environment to make sense of the world. Using the mental maps that we construct, we define rules, or heuristics, that act as shortcuts, enabling us to interpret our surroundings and make quick decisions. If we see a red light while driving a car, for example, our mind calls up patterns of knowing and enables us to act quickly.

There are dynamics in the brain that occur the second we turn our attention toward something. The thalamic reticular nucleus (TRN), a thin nucleus shield between the thalamus (the emotional center of the brain) and the cortex (the reasoning center of the brain), highlights all the neural circuits related to the object of attention and suppresses all distracting and irrelevant data.[208] In other words, when we perceive or act on information, stimulated axons must pass through the TRN, which in turn discerns what is and is not important and focuses and directs our thoughts and resulting actions to those which are essential.

Behavioral economist Daniel Kahneman defines this quick, intuitive, unconscious thinking as our "Type 1 System." Most everyday activities make heavy use of this primary system. The "Type 2 System," on the other hand, is the slow, calculating, conscious thought process that one might use when solving a difficult problem.[209]

From Kahneman's perspective, the big difference between Type 1 and Type 2 thinking is that Type 1 is fast and easy but very susceptible to systematic errors, whereas Type 2 is slow and requires conscious effort but is much more resistant to errors. There is a limited pool of resources to engage in complex thinking or intentional effort, so we often need to rely on our fast thinking to conserve cognitive resources for situations such as coping with stress, solving problems, or practicing self-control.[210]

See the illustration on the next page.

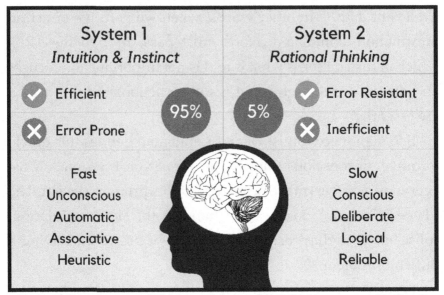

Fast and Slow Systems of Thinking: Type 1, or "fast" thinking, compared to Type 2, "slow" thinking.

Each of our fast-thinking systems is shaped by the cognitive maps that we have constructed over years of learning influenced by culture, family upbringing, education, and a myriad of other personal experiences. These maps form a basis for making decisions but also inherently introduce errors into our decision-making since we tend to be unaware of how our biases lead us to construct flawed narratives and arrive at incorrect conclusions.

The critical issue here is that when we subconsciously apply experience-based rules or heuristics to unfamiliar situations, we lose vital learning opportunities. The act of leveraging mental shortcuts without question or scrutiny has two effects: 1) We continue to unknowingly wear away our well-trodden neural pathways, further reinforcing faulty thinking patterns, and 2) We miss out on exercising the mental muscle of doing the hard work of thinking and learning.

Dozens of various types of biases have been documented in scientific literature. In fact, Wikipedia has accumulated a list of around 200 types of biases.[211] In *Unlocking Leadership Mindtraps: How to Thrive in Complexity*, Jennifer Garvey Berger nicely classifies biases into five common categories:[212]

Bias for Simplicity: We prefer easy stories and simple explanations. This goes back to our evolutionary bias to prioritize survival by filtering out unnecessary noise and conserving energy. We prefer a simple world of cause and effect, and we tend to make up simple narratives based on our own subjective reality.

Bias to Be Right: Also known as confirmation bias, we tend only to notice evidence of what we believe to be true. This bias leads us to see information that is only in agreement with our point of view. We embrace elements in our world that confirm our beliefs while ignoring those features that refute them. In times of change or disruption, this bias may prevent us from being mindful of all the information, including that which has changed and that which is new and causes us to make flawed decisions in our work and personal lives.

Bias to Belong: In our deep history, the bias to belong drives us to be part of a tribe and gain mental and physical support from a group of people. We are wired to be socially agreeable. We agree because we want to get along with—and be respected by—others who are like us. We also tend to pay more attention to and believe those who think like us, preventing us from seeing the perspective of others who are different from us. The perfect microcosm of this is found in our individual *social media bubbles*. We frequent those news and information sources that align with our thinking.

Bias for Control: We like to be in control of our world; it helps us feel safe. This is especially true in times of change. We pull in the reins on our thoughts or actions, or even information and new learning to at least *believe* we are in control. There is a tendency for some to completely shut down or ignore any information or events and happenings to maintain a sense of control.

Bias for Self-Identity: Our identity is a collection of mindsets that we form based on a lifetime of experiences and personal preferences. Also known as "self-serving bias," our bias for self-identity protects our ego and self-esteem. When our individual self-worth or identity is threatened, we tend to reframe facts to align with a view of the world that protects our beliefs about who we are.

Expertise

On February 1, 2003, the space shuttle Columbia disintegrated as it entered the Earth's atmosphere, killing all seven astronauts on board. NASA suspended space shuttle flights for more than two years as it scrutinized the disaster. According to the investigation report, Columbia was accelerating through 1,500 mph when a piece of foam about nineteen inches long by eleven inches wide and weighing about 1.7 pounds broke off from the external tank and collided with the left wing of the shuttle at about 545 mph.[213]

The report cited that the problem with foam had been known for years, but experts had dismissed the lightweight material as harmless. The investigation identified other issues as well, including deep-seated cultural and organizational practices that were detrimental to safety. The report also cited a reliance on past success as a substitute for sound engineering practice.[214]

Expertise is a type of cognitive bias deserving of its own examination because this mindset has repeatedly proven itself to be a significant hindrance to learning. It can make people overconfident with their intelligence and intuition and cause them to use Type 1 thinking when they should be using Type 2 thinking, as the space shuttle Columbia's foam example illustrates.

Perhaps surprisingly, the smartest people in the room are often the ones who have the most difficulty learning. Consider senior executives who have had successful career trajectories by attaining an ivy league education from a high-ranking school with best-in-class grades, then being hired by a top consulting firm where they were steadily promoted through the years. These very experts often have the most difficult time thinking about what could go wrong because they may not have had a lot of experience in their lives failing and then learning from their failures.

Moreover, when something does fail, experts can become defensive, ignore criticism, and blame others for failure. In short, an expert's ability to learn shuts down at the exact moment it is most needed.

Moral Convictions

There is another kind of cognitive bias that is so strong it requires specific attention, and that is moral conviction. Inarguably, moral conviction is at the root of many disagreements and can sometimes lead to political divides, social unrest, violence, and war. Moral conviction may be the most deep-rooted bias we have, and it's at the heart of what is polarizing much of worldwide politics.

Moral conviction is based on fundamental beliefs about what is right and what is wrong and causes us to be immune to what those with differing opinions believe or feel. In concert with other biases, moral conviction strengthens our sense of belonging within groups of like-minded people and can cause us to operate with a closed mind. But this closed mind doesn't necessarily apply to just the moral conviction at question. We can form new opinions entirely unrelated to the original belief, based on what others within or outside of our social bubble believe.

Linda Skitka, professor of psychology, the University of Illinois at Chicago, has conducted extensive research on the psychological characteristics and consequences of attitudes that are experienced as moral convictions. Her findings indicate that strong moral convictions are most often associated with:[215]

- Higher levels of political engagement such as voting or volunteerism

- Distancing from those who think differently

- Less good will and cooperativeness in attitudinally diverse groups

- Greater inability to find solutions to resolve disagreements

- Greater distrust of otherwise legitimate authorities to make the right decisions

- Rejection of decisions and policy outcomes

- Greater acceptance of vigilantism and violence to achieve morally convicted ends

Beliefs can create fixed mindsets that get in the way of learning, and the solution proposed by Skitka is to set aside profoundly held beliefs, even temporarily, and stand in another pair of shoes to develop a deeper, more comprehensive understanding of the situation or the policy or the person. The next chapter will go deeper into strategies to mitigate bias and open ourselves to learning.

Obstacles to learning come from many different aspects of our lives, and none of us are free of them. Where they most often impede is in our lack of motivation to learn, our cultural beliefs about failure, our tendency to let others do the hard work of learning, or as the result of our harboring cognitive biases that efficiently filter out information that is needed to learn. Overconfidence in what we already know, failing to examine our failures, or being immutable in our beliefs all get in the way of our learning.

While these barriers to learning can present significant challenges to our motivation and ability to learn, there are strategies we can use to shift our mindset, overcome these obstacles to personal growth, and open ourselves to learning in our adult life and well into old age.

7
Learning to Learn

"The illiterate of the 21st century will not be those who cannot read and write, but those who cannot learn, unlearn and relearn."

— Alvin Toffler

We can all agree that the COVID-19 pandemic upended the world as we knew it. Our familiar, patterned, comfortable lives changed virtually overnight, but we adapted and discovered new ways of accomplishing things, and in so doing, bolstered our ability to learn.

While we are hardwired with an unlimited potential to learn, the barriers revealed in the last chapter—the lack of motivation, free riding, ignoring failure, cognitive bias, expertise, and moral conviction—limit this capability for all of us. However, these limitations can be overcome with increased awareness and intention. We can *learn to learn*, thereby expanding our capabilities through strategies that shift our mindset.

Before I discuss the strategies to transform yourself into a life-long learner, it is helpful to examine a useful framework for adult development.

The Stages of Adult Development

Harvard psychologist Robert Kegan (1946-), first proposed a framework for understanding stages of adult cognitive growth through his Constructive Developmental Theory (CDT) in 1982.[216]

Each of the five stages defined in Kegan's framework represents an increasing capacity in adults for mental complexity as well as a growing awareness of how emotions and beliefs impact thinking and one's sense of identity:[217]

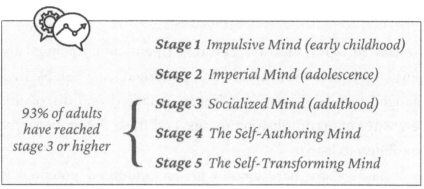

Stage 1 *Impulsive Mind (early childhood)*

Stage 2 *Imperial Mind (adolescence)*

93% of adults have reached stage 3 or higher

Stage 3 *Socialized Mind (adulthood)*

Stage 4 *The Self-Authoring Mind*

Stage 5 *The Self-Transforming Mind*

Kegan's Stages of Adult Development: Compared to other models of development that start in childhood and are designed to be attained by everyone, Kegan's model is specifically geared toward adults, who may or may not reach the fifth and final stage.[218]

Note that these stages are not referring to intelligence as measured by our IQ, but rather how we make sense of the world and operate within it. Although stage two primarily represents the adolescent years, a small percentage of adults never make it to stage three. Those individuals tend to harbor a mindset centered on their own needs and interests.[219] Most adults are somewhere at or between stages three to five, which is where I will focus this discussion.

Stage 3—The Socialized Mind

An individual who perceives the world through the Socialized Mind is influenced by the ideas, social and cultural norms, and belief systems of the people and social structures around them. Individuals in this stage tend to view themselves through the thoughts, beliefs, and morals expressed by others. They seek external validation to derive their sense of self. Those who have plateaued at this level of mental complexity tend to lack an independent, strong sense of self and are often more concerned with others' perspectives and assessment of who they are.

Stage 4—The Self-Authoring Mind

At this stage, adults begin to define who they are and how others or their environment see them. They understand that they are individuals with thoughts, feelings, and beliefs that are independent of the standards and expectations of others. They distinguish the opinions of others from their own sentiments to formulate their own thoughts and positions on things, people, and events. They develop an internal sense of direction and the resilience to create and follow their own course: *"This is who I am and what I believe."*

At this plateau, we question existing beliefs, the expectations and values of others, and take stands on causes. We solve social dilemmas and other problems with our own reasoning. And we find our own voice as we formulate and frame our own understanding of the world.

Stage 5—The Self-Transforming Mind

In stage five, one's sense of self is not tied to a particular identity or role, but rather is constantly shaped through the exploration of one's own self and through interactions with others. Individuals at this stage are intrigued by paradox, can hold contradictory viewpoints, and frame ideas and problems from multiple perspectives.

This concept of the brain being in a constant flux of this nature has been validated by recent neuroscientific studies that I highlighted in Chapter 5. And although we do not have a definitive answer yet as to exactly how consciousness relates to the brain, some cognitive scientists have begun to reference Buddhist thought in their research, which I will delve into more in Chapter 9.[220]

Those individuals nearing or plateauing at stage five are no longer constrained by their own sense of identity. They can step back from and reflect on the limits of their own ideology and hold multiple thoughts and ideologies at once. They understand things from many different perspectives. They comprehend the complexities of life, expand on who they are in the world, and continually reinvent themselves.

The chart on the next page illustrates the combined results of two large-scale studies (in 1987 and 1994) of the distribution levels of mental complexity among adults along the five stages of adult development.[221]

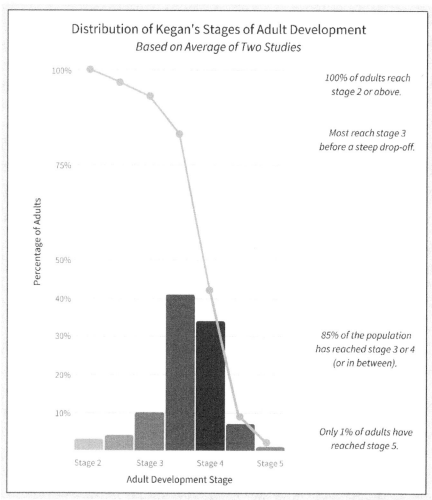

Kegan's Development Plateau: *While adults rarely fail to reach stage 3, developing the mental complexity required to reach stage 5 is quite rare. Many adults are between stages.*[222]

I am sharing this model for two reasons: 1) According to Kegan, growing as an adult is not as much about learning new information, facts, and knowledge as it is about *transforming the way we know and understand the world.*[223] I once heard Kegan describe this as enlarging versus filling the vessel known as our mind; 2) Given that the human brain is constantly growing and changing, virtually none of us have plateaued. There is room for all of us to learn, grow, and continue to advance as we age.

Cultivating a Learning Mindset

Becoming a learner begins with one's mindset. By understanding Kegan's framework of adult development and being aware of where we ourselves may lie within that framework, we can start to push past the barriers to learning and transition to higher stages of development. You can cultivate a learning mindset and establish a habitual practice around being open to learning through 4 key approaches:

1. **Connect to Purpose**—Link your goals and priorities to purpose and strengthen your ability to persevere.

2. **Learn From Experiences (Failure and Success)**— Incorporate cycles of learning into your daily living.

3. **Practice Unknowing**—Let go of existing knowledge so you can discover the new.

4. **See Yourself as Unfinished**—See yourself on a journey that is unending and set an ongoing intention to learn.

Simply increasing your awareness of these mindsets and approaches will begin to shift your perspective.

Connect to Purpose

Prioritizing learning for learning's sake can be difficult, especially when we are busy with our day-to-day lives. But when we are driven to a purpose, it affects how we live our lives and do our work. Cornell University psychologist

Anthony Burrow researches purpose. He defines purpose as an internally-driven quest and belief that life has a sense of direction, and he recommends considering purpose as an organizer for goals and priorities.[224]

You may have heard the origin story of Starbucks. At the age of seven, former CEO Howard Shultz witnessed what he now calls *"The fracturing of an American family."*[225] His father had sustained significant injuries from falling on the ice while working at a delivery job, and the lack of health care benefits and worker protections led to a considerable financial struggle for the family. Schultz confesses that this event profoundly influenced his purpose when he started Starbucks in 1987. Then CEO Howard Shultz wanted to build a company that his father never had a chance to work for, a company that values the dignity of every employee.

Purpose can drive us to do amazing things, but it can be difficult to maintain the right level of perseverance, particularly in the face of adversity. According to grit expert Angela Duckworth, to strengthen your ability to persevere, organize your objectives and goals into a hierarchy.[226] For example, suppose your purpose is to make the world a more visually beautiful place, and one of your goals is to cultivate a magnificent flower garden. In that case, your low-level goals, such as buying soil and planting flowers, would be at the very bottom of the hierarchy, supporting your overall goal.

Using Duckworth's hierarchy-of-goals thinking, you should focus your persistence on the broader purpose and less on goals and tasks, respectively. This can sometimes require though having to take a giant step back on your purpose. Consider

Shultz's purpose of creating a company for which his father never had the chance to work. If Schultz would not have received the necessary investment resources to grow Starbucks, the coffee chain may not exist as we know it today. Shultz would have failed in growing a coffee chain, but he could have continued to pursue his broader goal of building that kind of company, perhaps in some other way or some other place.

It might be helpful to think of your broader objective as a journey and reframe setbacks as necessary steps to achieve that broader purpose. It can help you "stick with it," but it can also help you tap into that intrinsic motivation or learn through failure. By connecting with your overarching purpose, you can persist through learning, knowing that it ultimately serves your overall objective. You can then begin to view life with a broader perspective and develop greater self-management and determination.

The Role of Gratitude

As you consider your purpose, pausing to be grateful for what you have attained can help cement your purpose and strengthen your patience to persevere. David DeSteno, a psychologist at Northeastern University, studies the role of emotions like gratitude in increasing the human virtue of patience.[227] In 2014, DeSteno and his colleagues conducted a study to determine which emotions had the greatest impact on self-control and patience.[228]

Study participants were randomly assigned to one of three emotion-generating conditions: grateful, happy, or neutral, and were asked to recall an event that made them feel grateful, an event that made them happy, or the events of a typical day (neutral). After participants spent five minutes writing about the assigned topic in detail, they were asked to score the intensity of their emotions (happy and grateful). They were then asked to make a series of choices between receiving a smaller cash amount immediately or a larger cash amount at a point from one week to six months in the future.[229]

The results show that if people are asked to think of something that they were thankful for beforehand, they are more willing to wait longer for more money. Thoughts of gratitude result in greater self-control and more patience.[230] This coincides with research that has already shown that gratitude heightens behaviors such as cooperation that favor long-term gain even at an immediate cost. DeSteno and his colleagues conducted additional studies, including one that shows that a daily gratitude practice can improve one's patience.[231]

According to Desteno, *"When you feel those emotions* [like gratitude], *they change what your mind values. It makes you value the long term more and what you find is that it just makes it easier to persevere toward your goals and to control selfish temptations."*

These results correlate to something discussed earlier in the book—the brain is not fixed. Even emotions like gratitude can alter your thinking and rewire your brain. That means self-control, and therefore patience and perseverance, are not fixed; we can develop these traits.

Purpose and Motivation

Connecting learning to a purpose can help overcome the barrier that lack of motivation poses by strengthening your intrinsic motivation to learn. By connecting learning to a purpose, the pinnacle of your goals hierarchy, you can approach learning a new skill or earning a degree as a journey of self-development. In addition, individuals who are purpose-driven not only exhibit a range of better health measures but there is evidence that having a purpose has cognitive benefits, including slower rates of cognitive decline and lower risk of Alzheimer's.[232]

As we learn about ourselves and practice gratitude for our progress along the journey, we strengthen our ability to learn through cultivating our ability to persevere in the face of challenges; we may be less apt to free ride and more willing to explore our biases and explore failure as part of the journey. Learning takes time, and reflecting on how you have learned and how it has enriched your life can feed your future learning.

Learn From Experiences (Failures and Successes)

We often think of failure as an opportunity to learn, but the problem is, as we learned in the last chapter, our brains do not always work that way. Not only do we tend to avoid investing time reflecting on our mistakes and general lack of success, but our brains are hardwired to avoid learning from failure. We *can* learn from failure and disappointment, but to do so, we have to intentionally override our hardwired reactions.

The Negativity Effect

While we tend not to learn from failure easily, our brains do spend cognitive energy on failure. Studies demonstrate that we tend to give greater weight to negative events and objects in our lives, including negative thoughts on personal traits. According to one study, the negativity of adverse events tends to be more impactful, urgent, and unfold and develop more rapidly than does the positivity of positive events.[233]

Another study revealed we give greater weight to bad events in everyday life. Physical trauma, breakdowns in interpersonal relationships, adverse childhood experiences, and poorly delivered feedback have a more significant impact than positive events. Additional findings show that negative information is processed more thoroughly than positive information. This is likely why we tend to be more motivated to avoid bad feedback and bad self-definitions than to pursue good ones, meaning we invest energy in avoidance rather than seeking.[234]

These studies indicate that the greater attention given to negative events encourages more brain activity. In the past, some researchers posited that this increased brain activity showed more learning, but there is also evidence that we do not learn well from failure. Why and how does failure undermine learning? There are several aspects in how failure affects our cognitive systems that, when brought together, may shed more light on how best to learn from our mistakes as well as our successes.

Feedback Failure

Although we try to embrace failures as teachable moments as a society, studies show that failure can undermine learning.[235] In a series of five studies by researchers at the University of Chicago, participants answered binary-choice questions, such as True-False questions. They were given feedback about whether they answered correctly or incorrectly, along with the correct answer. For example, a participant incorrectly answering "False" would receive the feedback "Incorrect. The correct answer is True." On follow-up tests, however, results showed that participants learned less from failure feedback than from success feedback. Participants who received failure feedback remembered fewer of their answer choices.[236]

The studies suggest that failure can cause people to tune out helpful information, even the correct answer. Yet, something different happened when participants observed others receiving negative feedback. They were able to learn from others' failures just as well as from others' successes. It turns out that *ego threat* interferes with our ability to learn from our own failures; reducing ego threat can help us accept and learn from failure.[237]

Cognitive Dissonance

Failure feedback creates cognitive dissonance, a mental conflict that occurs when new information contradicts what we believe about ourselves. For instance, the feedback *"you are incorrect"* counters *"I know this."* When negative feedback challenges our self-belief, we often try to reconcile that contradiction to what we know with explanations or reasoning that protects our ego, such as suggesting that the questions were poorly worded or that the questions were not relevant.

Neural studies enabled by advances in imaging technologies have recently identified key brain regions that play an important role in avoiding aversive outcomes when reconciling conflicting information. Cognitive dissonance shuts down the prefrontal cortex and activates the flight or fight response in the amygdala.[238] As a result, the brain disregards any information that could aid in learning from failure, and over time the person develops a defensive and self-protecting mindset.

Studies show that increased brain activity from negative thoughts is due to more internal rumination on our inadequacies and unfolds more rapidly in the mind. In this regard, a feeling of failure can immediately overwhelm all other thoughts. This begs the question: why are we so obsessed with learning from failure?

Failure and the Self-Transforming Mind

Consider Kegan and Lahey's stages of adult development presented at the beginning of this chapter. The self-transforming mind can comprehend changes that life brings and is comfortable with being wrong or failing. Being more expansive with their identity and open to self-reinvention, the self-transforming mind sees failure, along with success, as a part of life and something to embrace and understand.

John C. Maxwell wrote about this in his book, *Failing Forward: Turning Mistakes Into Stepping Stones for Success*, where he distinguishes successful people from ordinary people based on how they define and contend with failure. People are too quick to isolate events in their life and label them as failures and not see their mistakes and disappointments in the context of the bigger picture of life.

To make his argument, Maxwell defines failure by what it is not: it's not avoidable; it's not an event; it's not objective; it's not the enemy; it's not irreversible; it's not a stigma, and it's not final.[239] Instead, it is a process of life that we define for ourselves and can use to fertilize our growth. We can move forward by embracing a new definition, viewing failure as an inevitable price we pay to achieve success, no different from buying gas for a road trip.

Maxwell's teachings are not entirely new. In fact, similar thinking can be found in the Bhagavad Gita, a Hindu scripture dating back to somewhere between 400 BC and 200 AD. As the story goes, the deity Krishna advises prince Arjuna about what his mindset should be regarding events in his life: *"Treat success and failure, profit and loss, happy occurrences and unhappy ones just the same."*[240]

The Learning Cycle

One way to overcome the reptilian flight or fight response to negative feedback is to reflect on our experiences—both failures and successes—equally. David Kolb (born in 1939), known for his research on experiential learning, maintained that *"learning is a process whereby knowledge is created through transformation of experience."*[241] He created a framework for the learning cycle, a simple process whereby we transform experiences with the intent of extracting new ideas or principles to inform future actions for the better. Humans naturally reflect on experience, which alters our identity. Over time, this cycle repeats and transforms us.

Below is a four-step reflective model I adapted from Kolb's Learning Cycle:[242]

1. **Experience**—Complete a task or experience an event either first-hand or through a second-hand account.

    o   Recall the story of the Columbia disaster from the last chapter.

2. **Reflect**—Intentionally take a step back, observe the situation and results and ask yourself: What went well, what did not go well? What could have been better?

    o   Surmise that experts were clouded by their own knowledge. More collaboration, thorough analysis, and specific safety protocols could have yielded better results.

3. **Form principles and concepts**—Distill what you have learned into new information you can use for the future and share with others.

    o   Make broader generalizations, like "beware of over-confidence from experts" and "watch out for signs of groupthink."

4. **Test and learn**—Experiment with the new principles and concepts in new situations to see where they apply and do not apply.

o When you find yourself in situations where you may be the expert among many, question whether you need more data and facts or an outsider's view.

Note this is an iterative model that continues during and long after an event. Through this model, we can develop the resilience and adaptability to not only learn from success or others' failures but from our own failures, preparing us for similar situations in the future.

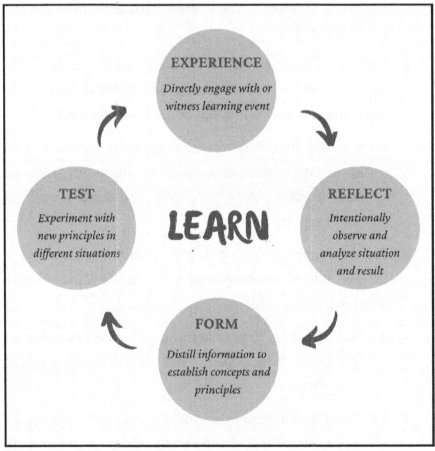

The Learning Cycle: Based on the principles of Kolb's learning cycle, this learning process represents learning as a perpetual process rather than a linear path.

Reflection as a Tool

Reflection is a tool for overcoming each of the barriers to learning mentioned in the previous chapter. Through awareness of the reflective learning cycle and applying reflection activity, we can understand our motivations, our tendencies to avoid the hard work of learning, and the various biases that get in the way of our understanding. Moreover, the practice of reflection and the formation of principles and concepts to test and learn from helps consolidate learning and forges new pathways in the brain.

Integrating daily reflection becomes a powerful tool for learning and building self-efficacy—the belief that what you do matters. The simple daily act of reflection will serve to reinforce that belief and thereby improve motivation to learn. We can break the barrier of ignoring and dismissing failure by making space for it and understanding its essential role in our learning.

Practice Unknowing

Looking again at the stages of adult development, consider that progression through each stage involves an increasing awareness of one's biases and assumptions of others. At stage three—the Socialized Mind—individuals don't fully understand and contextualize cognitive biases (both their own and others). Driven by their own sense of who they believe they are (bias for self-identity) and desire to fit in (bias to belong), they tend not to see themselves through the lens of biases.

Alternatively, an individual at stage five—the Self-Transforming Mind—is aware of biases (theirs and others) and can observe their behavior and examine its effects impartially. Kegan recently wrote that *"All evolution of consciousness as we understand it always involves moving what was a subject to an object. When you're subject to something, you can't see it."*[243] In other words, what was once something that you were unconsciously subject to (bias for self-identity), becomes something that you can look at, reflect on, and manage or control. Or you can simply think of it as self-awareness of who we are and what affects our being and thinking.

For example, a person who has reached stage five of adult development can hold moral convictions, understand why others hold different convictions, and recognize that both beliefs have merit. Stage five is characterized by holding a certain value as personally vital, yet accepting conflicting opinions and even empathizing with contradictory views.

Experiences Are the Wiring

Although genes provide the blueprint for the formation of brain circuitry, the complex design structure of the brain is built through a process that begins before birth and continues well into adulthood. In other words, we are born with a *genotype*, or genetic identity, but our phenotype, our observable traits, are shaped by our experiences. For example, we know that early experiences wire the neural foundation for all future learning, behavior, and health.[244]

According to modern brain scans, basic neural connections and skills form first, as early as the second trimester. More complex circuitry and skills develop in the first few years of life, with more than one million new neural connections forming every second during infancy. After this period of rapid growth, connections are then made more efficient through a process called pruning, which allows new brain circuits to develop and thicken.[245]

While the early years are the most active period for establishing neural connections, new connections can form throughout life as we prune unused connections to make way for new neural growth. It is impossible to determine what percentage of brain development occurs by a certain age, because differing genes and childhood environments influence the continuous process. More importantly, the early-life neural architecture serves as the foundation for future connections.

The following graph approximates the brain's ability to change in response to experiences.[246] As you can see, it takes far less effort to change in our youth than later in life. So, learning becomes more challenging with age; but, the question is, can we flatten the curve?

See the illustration on the next page.

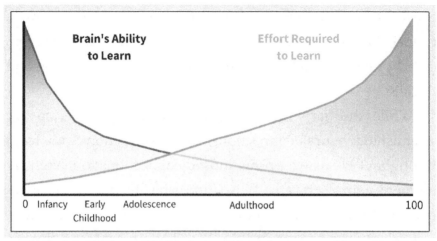

The Brain's Ability vs. Effort to Learn: Take one key term we all learned in 2020: "flattening the curve." There may be nothing we can do to stop the inevitable effects of aging. Still, we can slow it down, essentially dampening our perception of cognitive decline and keeping us mentally agile longer. [247]

Disrupting Our Matrix

What if we could increase the ability of our brains to change *and* reduce the amount of effort required to change it? Remember, the hardwiring of our brains, the cognitive schemata we each have developed over time, including our biases, are all part of our "personal matrix." Now imagine you can disrupt your personal matrix by "unknowing-it-all."

Disrupting our matrix and therefore being open to learning begins with awareness and *really* listening. Through awareness and simple intent, we can start to forge new pathways that encourage learning. Chapter 8 will dive deeper into tactics you can use to disrupt your personal matrix, but for now, these are four of my favorite strategies to become an *unknow*-it-all:

- *Practice Shoshin: Shoshin* is a word from Zen Buddhism that conveys receptivity, openness, and a lack of assumptions, biases, moral convictions, expertise, and other preconceptions. To practice Shoshin is to adopt a "beginner's mindset."[248] In other words, let go of what you already know—when you are free from your own knowledge, you are free to learn.

- *Turn off autopilot*: Remember that Kahneman refers to System 1 thinking as the *autopilot* that operates fast to make split-second decisions. System 1 thinking, which is based on shortcuts and heuristics, makes up 98 percent of our thinking, while System 2 thinking is deliberate and slow.[249] By slowing down and being more deliberate, we can engage our problem-solving system and overcome our preconceptions.

- *Recognize and embrace discomfort:* If you are guided by cognitive bias, it can be very uncomfortable to face challenges to our beliefs, as it threatens our sense of control. We are hardwired to protect our egos. Learning something new can mean admitting we have been misinformed or wrong, especially in adulthood when our knowledge feels immense and stable.

- *Question assumptions:* Each of us has a personal matrix built on our own unique experiences, which affect how we perceive and know the world. Once we are out of autopilot, we can examine our own assumptions and preconceptions and free ourselves to see others. Get used to asking yourself questions such as: *"What is different about this situation? Or is there another possible explanation?"*

Unknowing-it-all

Overcoming the barriers of bias, including expertise and moral conviction, means being intentional about creating space for that which you do not know. There are often clues when someone's thinking is limited by their own biases: *"It must be true, I heard it on the news."* Or *"I've seen this before; I know how it plays out."*

See the illustration on the next page.

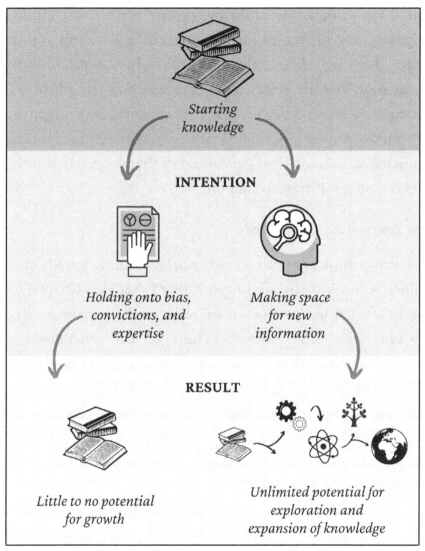

Creating space for what you do not know: Our knowledge, experience, and beliefs are cornerstones to our identity, so we don't often question them when they become obstacles. By intentionally creating space for the unknown, you invite the opportunity for knowledge beyond the scope of your previous experience.[250]

It is the practice of *not* knowing that helps us get to the other side of knowing. Not knowing breaks the barriers that are formed through the various cognitive biases, expertise, and moral convictions we build up in our adult lives. Further, ongoing new discoveries and the rewarding feeling you get from thinking differently can strengthen your intrinsic motivation to learn as you begin to realize how the practices of unknowing enrich your life and relationships. By being aware of yourself and your personal matrix and making space for new knowledge, you can develop a mindset that is open to learning and ongoing self-transformation.

See Yourself As Unfinished

We like to think of ourselves in the present tense. Recall Daniel Gilbert's "End-of-History Illusion" that I shared in Chapter 5— the belief that the person we are today is the person we were always meant to be. From that study, we can generalize that, despite acknowledging that their beliefs, preferences, and perceptions have evolved over time, most people believe they will not change in the future.[251] But people do change, and longitudinal studies indicate that ten years later, the same people will acknowledge that they have changed yet still see themselves as a *fait accompli*.

You might also remember that the adult brain continues to grow new neurons and forge new pathways, giving us an unending capacity to develop and grow. We can change. Moreover, once we see our "self" as a sort of gradual unfolding of who we are, we see that all that we can be is before us. Seeing yourself as an unfinished work in progress will allow you to change your mindset from "I am who I am" to "I am growing and evolving," which enables you to be open to ongoing transformation and re-invention.

Interestingly, when you see yourself as unfinished, you accept others as unfinished as well, enabling you to face those around you with an entirely new brand of compassion, one that will fuel others' learning as well. Everyone can learn, and it is never too late to learn.

Life-Long Learning

The mindsets explored in this chapter are table-stakes for learning. They help us overcome what are natural barriers to continual development and transformation well into adulthood.

And we do need to keep learning well into adulthood. The world has changed, and humans can and will step up to learn to deal with the challenges of the future and maintain relevance in a working world where machines increasingly accomplish tasks. In addition, the demands of a changing world and increasing complexity will require a growing need for humans to up our game, just as we have been doing for the last seven million years.

Now is the time for Human Intelligence (HI), developing the mental quality that enables us to learn from experience, adapt to new situations, deal with abstract concepts, and use knowledge to change and adapt to our environment. We need to be aware of our barriers to learning, overcome them, and become life-long learners.

See the illustration on the next page.

Connect to purpose / \ *Learn from experiences*

Connect your goals to a greater purpose.

- *Sustain motivation*
- *Foster gratitude and perseverance*
- *Inspire others*

Reflect on your successes AND failures.

- *Promote personal growth*
- *Reduce repetitive errors and reinforce continued success*
- *Compound learning potential*

Embrace the discomfort of unfamiliarity.

- *Reveal new insights*
- *Foster resilience*
- *Disrupt automatic processes that hinder growth*

You are a work in progress. Act accordingly.

- *Engender self-compassion*
- *Promote knowledge-seeking*
- *Overcome perceived limitations to learning*

Practice unkowing \ / *See yourself as unfinished*

Cultivate a Learning Mindset: *Remember that cultivating a learning mindset is an ongoing process to apply to all aspects of life. Try using these principles at work or on a particularly tough project and continue to reflect and utilize them with increasing success.*

Part 4

Becoming a Learner

8

Your Learning Practice

"We are what we repeatedly do."

— Aristotle

Thus far in the book, I have discussed ways we can overcome myths and barriers to learning, to shift our mindset so that we can embrace our inherently unlimited capacity to learn. In the last chapter, I discussed important strategies to change your mindset, including connecting to purpose, learning from success *and* failure, letting go of what is known to discover the unknown, and seeing yourself as a perpetual work in progress.

When we see ourselves as perpetually unfinished, we embrace and accept the ongoing work of self-improvement. We can deliberately travel the curve of adult development to understand more about the world and ourselves. When we see ourselves as a work in progress, the bounds of what we can do *always* lie ahead.

I always loved the concept of *a practice* that I discovered when I started doing yoga. At first, I didn't think twice about the word; after all, we "practice" sports, and I was primarily taking a yoga class for exercise. But as I continued to attend classes and eventually earned my teaching certificate, the lull of that profound word took root. The definition I developed in my own mind, quite possibly influenced by the spiritual and religious underpinnings of yoga, is nuanced from what you might find in the dictionary. I would define a practice as "the consistent and regular performance of an activity *so that you may discover and explore the bounds of your capability.*"

If you Google the word "practice," you will find an Oxford definition that is, perhaps necessarily, reductive. It is not enough to say that a practice is a habitual activity or way of doing something; practice is grounded in intent. Consider that when my puppy begs for food at the dinner table, it is a habitual activity but not a practice, because practice is grounded in intent. That said, to say that the *only* intent is around improving proficiency does not land well either. Should I not practice yoga if I am getting older and not necessarily "better?"

Becoming a learner is to practice learning. That intent can be about becoming increasingly better or more skilled at something, but it can also simply be a process of discovery or observation. When we practice something, there is no endpoint; instead, our abilities slowly unfold, and we continually uncover new understanding or skill, as if some hidden gems are tucked into the countless folds in our brains. Learning is the practice of living.

So, how do you start embracing learning and become a learner? This chapter dives into some specific actions you can take to get started on the path of learning through three simple steps:

1. **Set a learning intention**—Set objectives aligned to your purpose to ignite your passion and flip the switch on your motivation.

2. **Systematize your practice**—Commit to learn and build a habit around learning, including reflection.

3. **Cultivate a sense of wonder** (and embrace the suck)— Approach each day with curiosity and wonder; challenge what you think you know and gain comfort in discomfort.

Once you have a plan and start your practice, you will discover in Chapter 10 some learning hacks to help you tap into the abundant learning opportunities all around you.

Set a Learning Intention

In Chapter 6, I spoke of the barriers to learning, with lack of motivation being the foremost obstacle. I cited Ryan and Deci's years of research in intrinsic motivation and self-determination in human behavior that reveals that we are most deeply engaged and do our most creative work when we feel that we are acting according to our own will on behalf of goals that we personally find meaningful. Will and meaning are at the heart of adult learning theory: we only learn when we want to.

One of the four strategies we discussed in the last chapter was connecting to purpose. Through connecting to purpose, we can overcome motivational barriers to learning. By understanding the broader goal of who we want to be, we spark our own curiosity and aspirations so that learning feels rewarding, not like a chore.

Furthermore, by setting our sites on a broad goal, we can bank resilience that stands up in the face of minor setbacks. For example, suppose my goal is to help people discover and attain the farthest reaches of their own capabilities through learning. In that case, I may fail at, say, becoming a triathlon coach but perhaps succeed in some other way, like writing a book that shares what I have learned about lifelong learning.

The key takeaway then is that we are most motivated to learn when we are autonomously acting in a coherent way with our underlying interests or passions and when we are learning in service of our broader purpose.

The Concept of Life-Crafting

So, you might ask: *How do I discover my purpose?* To the young people reading this: no, that does not mean that you should already know exactly who you are. Truly, if there is one thing I know, it is that we often go about finding and setting our purpose way too late in life. Setting a purpose is something we should be doing early in life and revisit often, as our purpose is likely to take different shapes over the course of our lives.

Also, we can have more than one purpose—I may have an audacious altruistic goal while having another goal rooted in something I am passionate about. There are no rules to discovering your "why" except that it's something that ignites your intention to learn. It's easy to feel apprehensive about selecting a purpose, as if committing to a path renders others unwalkable. But a lack of purpose is the absence of any path at all, and you can always wander off or pave a new one. Often, we don't make a choice when we are unsure, but in reality, making any choice would be better than continuing to avoid it.

One concept that has resonated with me and incorporates the breadth of science around the topic is the concept of *life-crafting*, developed by Professor Michaéla Schippers and researcher Niklas Zielger, at the Rotterdam School of Management.

Schippers and Ziegler define life crafting as:

> *"A process in which people actively reflect on their present and future life, set goals for important areas of life—social, career, and leisure...and undertake actions to change these areas in a way that is more congruent with their values and wishes."*[252]

To discover your "why," start by reflecting on your:

1. **Values**—As you reflect on your past, present, and future, what are the key values you want to model?

2. **Passions and interests**—What makes you feel most inspired and alive?

3. **Current and desired skills and competencies**—What are your strengths, and what strengths would you like to further develop?

4. **Career interests**—What kind of career path do you want?

5. **Social life**—When it comes to relationships, what energizes and de-energizes you? What kind of friends and family life would you like to have?

6. **Your ideal future state**—Consider what aspects of life come to mind. Those are what is important to you.

As you reflect on these things, you can begin to craft a narrative, a vision board, or some other creative "life-crafting deliverable" (like a magazine cover with you as the cover photo). Developing a view of a specific and ideal future state not only sows seeds of purpose, but it also leads to "increased levels of self-regulation, resilience, self-efficacy, and engagement."[253]

Systematize Your Practice

James Clear, the author of *Atomic Habits* and expert on habit formation, wrote, "You do not rise to the level of your goals. You fall to the level of your systems," meaning that you might have a big audacious goal, but you need a system or a process to achieve it.[254] As with any practice, the more deliberate and intentional we are, the more likely we will have a consistent and effective practice. By making firm commitments to learn and building a habit around learning, we can systematize our own learning practice and make it just as much a part of our lives as brushing our teeth or eating breakfast.

The Power of Commitment

In 2016, I decided to complete an Ironman in Arizona the following year. I began to be an Ironman to make sure I did not back out: I paid the sign-up fee, posted my intention on social media, and shared the news with everyone I knew, including my family, friends, and work colleagues. I bought an Ironman

Arizona backpack for my training gear and started carrying that to the gym. I established a detailed 24-week training plan, and I joined social media groups to find other would-be Ironmen with whom I could connect.

These activities served a purpose: they helped me establish the identity I had decided to adopt and created a situation in which backing out now was no longer an option. I had created a self-imposed reality where I had no choice but to become an Ironman.

Popularized by Freakonomics co-authors Stephen Dubner and Steven Levitt, the concept of a *commitment device* was first used by game theory economist and Nobel Laureate Thomas Schelling in 1956.[255,256] Schelling used the term *precommitment device* to describe the mechanisms for restraining future choices by making one choice—the choice to follow through on a commitment—the optimal choice.[257]

So, to make it *really* difficult for me to back out on my plan to be an Ironman, I had developed *many* commitment devices. And they worked. I stuck to the plan, and in November of 2017, I had the amazing life experience of hearing the official voice of Ironman and Hall-of-Famer Mike Reilly tell me, "Teri Hart, you are an Ironman."

We all have an inherent desire to be (and to appear) consistent with what we have already done or intend to do. In essence, this is to preserve our own identity and sense of who we are (recall Bias for Self-Identity from Chapter 6). Once we have made a choice or declared our position on something, we face and even manufacture personal and social pressures to compel us to act consistently with that commitment and behave in ways that justify our earlier decision.

Dean Karlan, the founder of Stickk.com and Professor of Economics and Finance at Kellogg School of Management at Northwestern University, discovered the power of what he refers to as a "Commitment Contract," a binding agreement you make with yourself. Through personal experience and academic research, Karlan found that people were significantly more successful if they made a binding commitment to achieve their goals. On Stickk.com, users make a commitment and can set a commitment device by donating to a charity if they fail to live up to their terms of the agreement.

Once you have set an intention to learn, backing that up with commitment devices can help you kickstart your practice. Following through on your intention to learn can also start with a few simple steps.

Building Your System

Building a learning practice requires building a development system, or in other words, making a habit of learning. Habit formation expert James Clear advocates that the way to build habits is to get just one percent better each day—something that sounds almost too easy to do yet builds a firm foundation for continual improvement. Just wanting to play the piano will not help you become a pianist. Having a system or process in place for learning is what will help you achieve your goal. It is the "plan for implementation that makes the process effective," according to Clear.[258]

In an episode of Whitney Johnson's podcast *"Disrupt Yourself,"* Clear discussed some practices that help develop strong habits, including a few that I think are particularly effective for building a habit around learning:[259]

1. **Just show up.** Practicing the fundamental decision to "show up" for the activity for which you are building a habit can train you to overcome your objections and actually start. You can make a simple commitment to "show up" by doing something simple such as opening a book each day and reading at least one page.

2. **Vocalize what you are doing.** Hearing yourself say what you are about to do makes you actively conscious of the actions you are taking and prompts you to make a conscious decision to continue that action. For example, I say, "I am learning French a little bit each day," as I play Paul Noble's *Learn French*.

3. **Be specific about your intention.** Developing a practice requires that you are both deliberate about what you are doing and specific about how and when you are doing it. That is because specificity helps reinforce your identity and create commitment, as discussed earlier. "I meditate for 5 minutes every morning after drinking my first cup of coffee."

4. **Reflect on your progress.** Look for and create ways to track your progress to see how far you have come and motivate yourself to continue. For example, if your goal is to read 20 books a year, you might use Goodreads to

track your annual reading. If you are trying to improve a skill like golf, you might record a "before" video and others at various intervals. Looking back at your improvement will incent you to learn more.

5. **Focus on frequency and consistency over intensity to develop a practice**. It can be difficult to prioritize the time for something, particularly when you do not yet have a clear understanding of the benefit. By starting out with a small but frequent commitment, you can establish a practice that you can build on later. When I worked at McKinsey, the managing partner established a practice of "5 at 5," which meant 5 minutes of learning at 5pm *every day*. Frequency over intensity makes it easier to prioritize and starts to develop and strengthen your practice.

The Act of Reflection

Reflection is critical to learning, and ongoing cycles of reflection can help us push through to the next stage of adult development. There is no ego to protect when you are in a conversation with yourself. In reflective thought, you can challenge your assumptions and question your belief systems and knowledge. You can think deeply and draw connections among seemingly unrelated things.

Neuroscientists emphasize that intentional reflective thinking is key to "cementing" learning and enhancing your practice of the new knowledge, retention, and recall. It does so by facilitating patterning: how the brain searches for repetitions and groupings of thought streams and memories. Learning takes place when the brain uses these patterns and attaches meaning to them.[260]

Researchers are discovering that knowledge increases through reflective thinking and pattern recognition and by matching new information to memories. This creates more extensive neural networks. Positron Emission Tomography (PET) scans show that when people are given new information, their brains activate the stored memory banks. When these connections are made through reflective thinking, neural pathways are formed and thickened, and long-term memory is enhanced.

Cultivate a Sense of Wonder (and Embrace the Suck)

When was the last time you felt a deep sense of wonder? Approaching life with a sense of wonder means having curiosity and looking at the world around us through fresh eyes. My favorite example of looking at an ordinary thing with wonder comes from Walt Whitman's "Leaves of Grass:"

> *A child said What is the grass? fetching it to me with*
> *full hands;*
> *How could I answer the child? I do not know what it*
> *is any more than he.*

Whitman then goes on to postulate all the things grass could be from "a child itself" to the "beautiful uncut hair of graves."

How do you bring this sense of wonder and child's mindset to your daily life? While it's hardly an exact science, here are three ideas I've learned over the years:

1. **Slow down**—pause and take time to see what is around you.

2. **Be curious and ask questions**—seek to understand more than what is on the surface.

3. **Consciously look for new information**—what don't you know about the scene before you?

Cultivating a sense of curiosity and wonder can be a catalyst for many things: it generates positive motivations; it accelerates learning; it uncovers multiple possibilities when solving problems; it feeds and generates new brain cells well into our old age; and it has the potential to increase our happiness, which helps us build a habit of gratefulness. Approaching the world with curiosity and wonder, or at least allowing it to be part of your daily experience, can feed a growth mindset and make you happier and healthier in every aspect of your life.

Comfort with Discomfort

The phrase "Embrace the suck" originated around 2003 during Operation Iraqi Freedom. According to veteran Austin Bay, *Embrace the suck* is a quip that basically means "Face it, soldier. I've been there. This ain't easy. Now let's deal with it."[261]

As we engender curiosity and bring a sense of wonder into our daily living, we will, no doubt, find ourselves struggling and feeling "the suck." A personal experience that comes to mind is learning to ski. I learned to ski at an age when falling is considered more dangerous and therefore more uncomfortable. It is not fun to fall when you are not sure if you will be able to get up, or worse, break something. It is not fun to lose control going down a hill, particularly if there are other skiers below you, or trees…or a cliff.

Skiing is an apt metaphor. You cannot learn to ski and be in 100% control of the experience. It is difficult to learn to ski without fear, particularly as we get older. It is impossible to learn to ski without trying and failing; it's impossible to learn to ski without falling.

As humans, we generally avoid being uncomfortable. It is one of the reasons why I have spent many years in corporate learning and development, eschewing the results of learner reaction surveys on which we ask questions like *"Would you recommend this training to a colleague?"* or *"Was the training valuable?"* The response skews positive, especially if the program was the result of a promotion, a "high-potential" selection process, or was held at a resort on the beach. *Of course, that was the most amazing learning experience ever—way better than cramming for finals in a 100-year-old dorm room.*

Proof points of results are harder to come by, particularly in leadership development. But leadership development, if it is working, *should be uncomfortable.* We all should have to wrestle with those things that make us less good at leading than we could be: our armor, biases, and lack of empathy or compassion. The best leaders I know are willing to spend a lot of time being uncomfortable and exploring how to be better. Often, it takes time before we can look back at those uncomfortable experiences and find them valuable.

And like those leaders, you can create space for discomfort and accept that discomfort with equanimity. Being comfortable with discomfort is about recognizing when something is uncomfortable and accepting it as part of the process of growing and learning. When I am going through an uncomfortable learning experience, I often envision myself on a ski lift and tell myself it's OK to fall.

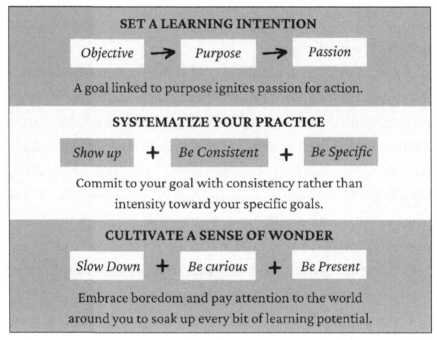

Learning as a Practice: Once you've cultivated a learning mindset, maintaining an intentional practice will solidify your ongoing learning potential.

Exploring our ZPD

Russian Psychologist Leo Vygotsky coined the phrase *Zone of Proximal Development* (ZPD) to describe the edge of our capability for learning. He defined it as "the distance between the actual developmental level...and the level of potential development"[262] that can be attained with assistance. In other words, our unique ZPD is the edge of our capabilities, and ongoing exploration of that edge gently expands the boundaries of who we are and what we can do.

When we take steps to practice learning—through setting an intention, systematizing our practice, and cultivating a sense of wonder—we slowly expand the boundaries of our ZPD and become lifelong learners.

9

Aligning Body and Mind

"It is through the alignment of the body that I discovered the alignment of my mind, self, and intelligence."

—BKS Iyengar

I would be remiss if I wrote a book about learning and represented it as a purely cerebral activity while neglecting the role of health and well-being. The idea that learning is something that requires mind, body, and spirit has been a deeply personal revelation for me. How we show up every day—for ourselves as well as for others—depends on our *whole selves* and not what is just in our cognitive capacity. *Self-efficacy*, or the belief that what we do matters, is not only derived from accomplishments, experiences, and the encouragement we receive; it is also derived from our physiological state or the condition and health of our bodies.[263]

In Chapter 7, I introduced four out of six strategies to help you create a learning mindset in yourself: (1) Connect to purpose; (2) Learn from experience; (3) Practice unknowing; (4) See yourself as unfinished and on an interminable journey of learning. There is so much evidence that supports the idea that simply increasing your awareness of these strategies will begin to shift your mindset and help you see the world with fresh thinking.

One additional strategy that requires ongoing intention is to (5) Optimize your health and well-being. This might seem logical because it makes sense to nourish and protect our bodies for our life's journey. But more than that, we are learning that we can, through healthful strategies, boost neurogenesis, or the creation of new brain cells, enhance memory and cognition, and slow down the brain's aging process. On the other hand, lack of health and well-being can cause your brain to decline faster and lead to problems that can compound learning challenges, like headaches, depression, and stress.

Learning as a lifelong activity can be realized to its fullest potential only if we are optimizing our cognitive function. To that end, we need to understand the implications of aging and stress on the brain and understand what we can do more of to enhance our ability to sustain learning well into old age.

The Aging Brain

As we get older, our ability to learn decreases. We are unable to recall information as easily, our working memory declines, and our information-processing abilities slow down.[264] Degradation of the brain, particularly how specific morphological changes lead to noticeable problems, is not well-understood. Specifically, researchers have often found it difficult to discern what changes in the brain indicate disease versus those due to normal aging.

Just like the long-held belief that neurogenesis halted upon reaching adulthood, researchers long held that aging triggers extensive loss of nerve cells. We now know that while normal aging does cause neuron loss, it is not as widespread as once thought—and neurogenesis continues, albeit at a slower rate.[265] There is, however, mounting evidence that, as we age, our neurons undergo increasing rates of *dendritic retraction*, which leads to loss of synapses.[266] Dendrites, you might recall, are the tiny branching structures through which a neuron receives electrochemical signals from other cells. Where these branches are shrinking and detracting, there is diminished activity in brains cells through reducing the number of synapses on the dendrites. (Note that this retraction is a normal process as *dendritic pruning* happens throughout our lives as part of learning.)

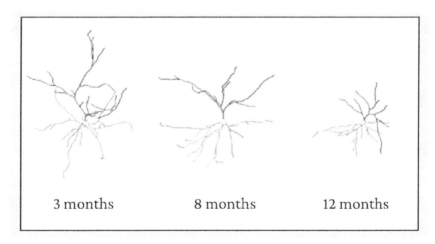

| 3 months | 8 months | 12 months |

Dendritic Retraction: *Dendritic pruning occurs regularly to maintain a healthy brain, retracting at an accelerated pace as the brain ages. Researchers study these effects in a specific population of mice called Senescence-Accelerated Mouse (SAM), who age early and rapidly.*[267]

In addition to accelerated dendritic retraction, the number of axons decreases. The myelin sheath, the fatty substance surrounding the axons, undergoes demyelination, decreasing the rate at which impulses are passed along the axon.[268] Aging is also associated with reductions in cortical thickness, white-matter integrity, neurotransmitter activity, and functional engagement in brain regions such as the hippocampus.[269]

The Role of Telomeres

Hundreds of causes are implicated in increasing the effects of aging on the brain. Studies suggest that the result of aging is at least partly linked to our telomeres, the protective caps of proteins at the ends of each strand of DNA that safeguard chromosomes from being worn down in each round of DNA replication.[270] The function of a telomere is to stop the ends of chromosomes from fraying or sticking to each other, much like the plastic tips on the ends of shoelaces keep laces from unraveling.

Each time a cell divides, these protein tips get shorter. Once telomere length reaches a particular point, the cell becomes subject to deterioration or more susceptible to disease.[271] If telomeres become so short that the genes they protect could be damaged, the cell stops dividing and renewing. This process of DNA replication or non-replication is one of the ways in which we age.[272]

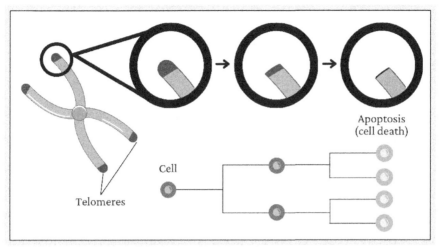

Telomeres: *Telomeres undergo "normal wear and tear" during replication, triggering cell death when their length reaches a critical point.*

Further studies implicate lifestyle choices and their role in shortening our telomeres and thereby accelerating the aging process. Poor diet, sedentary lifestyles, obesity, smoking, exposure to pollution, and alcohol consumption, as well as psychological factors such as stress and depression, all put the DNA of our cells at risk of damage, hastening the aging process and increasing the risk of disease.[273]

Telomere length is today regarded as an indication of the biological age of a person in contrast to their chronological age. That is to say, between two people of the same chronological age, the person with shorter telomeres has an increased risk of developing age-related diseases such as Alzheimer's or cancer and even possibly a shorter life expectancy.[274]

The Stressed-Out Brain

Some of the effects of stress on learning and the brain may be obvious to most of us. How can you possibly learn if you are under stress? Through science, we are learning that the effects of chronic stress not only impact learning during moments of stress but they can have a lasting impact on the health of the brain.

One of the most researched stress-induced changes in the brain is related to dendritic retraction.[275] Recall that dendritic retraction reduces the number of synapses. Studies have shown that when we are under stress, dendritic retraction (and therefore synapse reduction) occurs in the prefrontal cortex and parts of the hippocampus, areas of the brain responsible for thinking and learning.[276]

On the flip side, similar studies show that chronic stress *enhances* dendritic formation in the amygdala, the area of our brain responsible for the flight or fight response.[277] All this means that chronic stress has lasting effects by strengthening the neuronal pathways responsible for our stress-response while weakening pathways in the areas of our brain responsible for thinking and learning.

So, if you are a victim of chronic stress, the neurophysiological response stays on. There is a sort of *remodeling* of our brain. Over time, ongoing stress can impair memory recall and reduce the size of the hippocampus.[278]

One of the most significant areas of study of how stress affects the brain is the mental health condition of Post-Traumatic Stress Disorder (PTSD). Trauma expert Bessel van der Kolk has spent thirty years working with PTSD survivors. In his book, *The Body Keeps the Score*, he reveals how this re-wiring affects our lives—specifically areas related to control, engagement, and trust.[279]

Typically, our brain's adaptive response to stress leads to action. Our basic impulse to protect ourselves is automatic and unconscious, yet trauma can overwhelm this healthy response. As a result, traumatized people often get stuck in a state of powerlessness. Powerlessness limits the involvement of their prefrontal cortex, keeping their thinking brain disconnected, while their limbic system remains in charge, secreting stress hormones. As van der Kolk puts it, *"PTSD is the body continuing to defend against a threat that belongs in the past."*[280]

Countering Aging and Stress

While the effects of aging are somewhat inevitable, ongoing stress, which can be the result of many experiences from anxiety and depression to traumatic events, also has lasting impacts on the brain, and therefore our ability to learn. The good news is that we do have the ability to slow down and possibly reverse the impacts of aging and stress through health and well-being.

We all know that eating a healthy, balanced diet accompanied by regular exercise is fundamental to maintaining one's physical and mental health and well-being. For many of us, diet and exercise are the two areas we have the most control over when it comes to staying healthy. Not only are these effective in preventing excess weight gain, but healthier lifestyles are also associated with improved sleep and a positive mood.

There are vast resources available for anyone who wants to improve their health. My intent is to share some research and curated thoughts that demonstrate how what we do can affect our brains and how we think and learn.

Exercise and Nutrition

Studies have shown that good nutrition and aerobic exercise can reduce *and even reverse* losses in cognitive function, including learning and memory. While we have only begun to scratch the surface on the underlying causes for these improvements, we have known for some time that physical activity, in combination with a healthy lifestyle, improves blood flow to the brain. For example, studies conducted by Dean Ornish, founder of the Preventive Medicine Research Institute, showed that when you eat healthier, manage stress, exercise, and love more, your brain receives more blood flow and oxygen, improving overall cognitive function.[281]

More recent studies have begun to shed light on the underlying mechanisms. One study investigating the relationship between physical activity and glucose metabolism (necessary for cellular growth and maintenance) in late-middle-aged adults found that the intensity of physical activity is an important contributor to neuronal function. Moderate activity is the most beneficial overall, while vigorous physical activity has the most significant positive effect on the hippocampus and memory recall.[282]

In another study on aged dogs, researchers found that exercise improves memory consolidation and overall cognitive function.[283] Memory consolidation is a "process by which recently learned experiences are transformed into long-term memory."[284] In the study, the improvements were noticeable when performing memory consolidation learning tasks at 24 hours post-exercise (and not immediately after exercise). Furthermore, the benefits continued with ongoing, regular exercise, showing improvements after two weeks in *different* learning tasks. This suggests that there are potentially both short and long-term cognitive advantages of exercise.[285]

Similar studies have shown the benefits of nutrition, and we are starting to learn more about these underlying mechanisms as well. Perhaps the most well-established of these is the role of docosahexaenoic acid (DHA) in brain health. The research is voluminous. Diets high in DHA (also known as Omega-3 fatty acid, found in high amounts in fish) have been shown to *reverse* age-related changes in the brain and protect against Alzheimer's disease.[286] The role of DHA in learning and memory is equally compelling; supplementation with DHA has been shown to grow dendritic spines and spur neurogenesis in the hippocampus for learning and memory processing, among other things.[287]

While eating the right foods might be beneficial, there is also some evidence that a poor diet has a negative impact on the brain and learning. A meta-analysis of studies on rats showed that a diet high in fat and/or sugar harmed memory and spatial learning and memory across a range of hippocampus-related tasks.[288] One study, in particular, found that a diet high in fat and refined sugar influenced brain structure and function by reducing factors that regulate the development and maintenance of neuronal cells in the hippocampus, resulting in reduced plasticity and reduced capacity to learn and remember.[289] What's more is that the effects of a poor diet and aging together produce more significant impairments, leading to cognitive deficits.[290]

East Meets West

In the West, we are increasing our scientific understanding of how practices based on eastern philosophy benefit the brain. Our mind and well-being are inextricably linked, and I am writing this at a time of unprecedented convergence of western science and eastern philosophy.

Perhaps at the leading edge of this convergence are Daniel Goleman, psychologist and science journalist, and Richard Davidson, Founder of the Center for Investigating Healthy Minds and Director of the Waisman Laboratory for Brain Imaging and Behavior at the University of Wisconsin-Madison. Their recent collaboration: *Altered Traits: Science Reveals How Meditation Changes Your Mind, Brain, and Body*,[291] is based on a lifetime of work pursuing a scientific basis for the benefits of meditation.

Goleman and Davidson's findings, based on decades of research, reveal the mind-brain-body benefits of meditation:

- The amygdala shows dampened activity after only thirty hours of mindfulness-based stress reduction (MBSR)[292] practice, and daily practice appears to lessen ongoing stress reactions.[293]

- As little as two weeks of mindfulness practice was sufficient to significantly increase focus and working memory to boost Graduate Record Exam (GRE) scores.[294]

- At age 50, long-time meditators, compared with nonmeditators, had brains that were, on average, 7.5 years younger.[295]

- Meditation has been shown to increase telomerase activity, an enzyme that helps preserve the length of telomeres, thereby decelerating cellular aging.[296]

What I find most compelling in Goleman and Davidson's exhaustive research is stated in the title of the book—*Altered Traits*. Meditation can profoundly alter who we are. The ability to alter our traits opens a world of possibilities for learning and unlearning; we can change ourselves and our minds in ways we never thought possible.

One key tool of mindfulness-based stress reduction (MBSR) is yoga. The term yoga comes from the Sanskrit word "yuj," which means "to bind, join, attach and yoke, the powers of all the body, mind and soul to God," according to yogi Mahadev Desai.[297] Dating back thousands of years, yoga is one of the six orthodox systems of Indian philosophy and involves *integration of* the mind, body, and spirit through the practice of *asana* (physical postures) and breathwork.[298]

Yoga therapy is increasingly being leveraged to help those facing a variety of health conditions manage their symptoms, increase energy, and improve their mindset.[299] Yoga practice correlates with both improvement in measures of psychological resilience and improved vagus nerve regulation.[300]

The vagus nerve, specifically the dorsal vagal complex (DVC), provides the primary vagal motor fibers to organs below the diaphragm, the viscera, and digestive tract. This nervous circuit, related to our survival instinct, is the most primitive nervous circuit in our bodies from an evolutionary perspective.[301] When we sense imminent danger, the DVC is responsible for reducing cardiac output to reserve metabolic resources and alter bowel and bladder function. Habitual stress kicks the system into *overdrive*. And it's not designed to be in action consistently. Through breathwork and asana, we can regulate the DVC response to stress.[302]

Van der Kolk asserts that internal self-regulation of our thinking and emotional brains *requires* connection with the body through therapeutic interventions and activities such as meditation and yoga. These practices recalibrate the nervous system to allow the prefrontal cortex—the brain's "watchtower"—to monitor our body's reactions to stress more effectively. Therefore, mindfulness—knowing what you feel and understanding why—is helpful in strengthening the prefrontal cortex.[303] It allows us to understand and override a potentially stressful event with conscious awareness—essentially, to unlearn trauma.

Learning and Sleep

We spend nearly one-third of our lives sleeping, but *why we sleep* isn't entirely clear. While some researchers have posited it is to conserve energy or repair cells, these things could arguably be achieved in a restful but still conscious state. Our necessity for a state of unconsciousness has a few plausible explanations, one of which I believe has the most merit: sleep is for our brains.

And while we are still learning about the impact of sleep on the brain, evidence is accumulating that sleep is essential to learning. In fact, a meta-analysis reviewed a decade worth of research and cited growing evidence that sleep plays a role in *offline* memory processing.

To understand more about how sleep plays a role in memory processing, it is important to first understand the role of memory. Recall the Hebbian learning principle, "neurons that fire together wire together." At the neuronal level, learning strengthens (or weakens) synapses in the brain, creating a neural activation pattern. This rewiring, or *synaptic consolidation,* is essentially what makes our brains malleable, or plastic.[304]

Plasticity presents a problem, though: memories formed by these neural connections are not stable. To protect our memories for lasting learning, we need a place to store them— a physical trace known as an *engram.* According to recent research, some types of memories are stored through a two-stage process where new *episodes* are first encoded in the hippocampus and then repeatedly replayed to the neocortical system.[305] As this replaying is interleaved with other memories and experiences, memories form in the cortex.[306]

While we are still seeking to understand the role of sleep in memory more completely, we know that sleep enables this process of memory rehearsal, resulting in strengthening and consolidation of memories and an ongoing reorganization based on new information.[307] In other words, the brain is not merely storing new memories but making new sense of the world through interleaving new information with existing knowledge, providing the potential to generate novel understanding. If this is true, we are learning in our sleep and perhaps even devising creative ideas as we consolidate memories and compare old information with new.

Moreover, it is possible we can learn new information while sleeping. Research from 2020 uncovered that the brain is capable of a sort of *unconscious encoding*. Participants were taught fake foreign language words (like "topher") and their meanings while sleeping. Upon waking, participants correctly guessed the word meanings at a higher rate than would be due to chance alone, even though they had no conscious memory of learning the word.[308] Furthermore, functional magnetic resonance imaging (fMRI) revealed activation in brain areas associated with retrieval of the new information.[309]

This finding leads to some potentially far-reaching implications about learning and sleeping. Could we leverage sleep to improve learning? I will discuss more about how we might do that in the next chapter.

As you might infer, lack of sleep, or sleep restriction, can cause problems with learning, not only because there is a lack of opportunity for memory consolidation but also because it can cause damage to the brain. In one study, findings indicated that sleep restriction reduced neuronal pathways and rewiring, which could lead to functional impairment.[310] Other studies cite improved academic performance with better sleep.

In addition to the important role sleep plays in learning, sleep enables a sort of deep-cleaning cycle. The brain's glymphatic system, a network of vessels in the central nervous system (CNS), clears waste during sleep.[311] The glymphatic system also helps distribute glucose, amino acids, growth factors, and other essential compounds throughout the brain.[312]

Scientists also reported that the glymphatic system helps remove a toxic protein called beta-amyloid from brain tissue.[313] Beta-amyloid is known for accumulating in the brains of patients with Alzheimer's disease, forming amyloid plaques that can help diagnose the disease posthumously. Additional studies have shown that levels of beta-amyloid in the brain decrease during sleep.[314]

Coming from a Place of Compassion

The evidence is striking. Learning—and therefore our cognitive function—is not just a product of how we use our brains but also how we take care of ourselves, both mind and body. I realize that while this sounds simple, it's easier said than done. I also realize that there is still so much we do not know and possibly much more that can never be known.

While this was an exciting chapter for me to research, I never lost sight of how these words could spark controversy and judgment. This chapter is not intended to pass judgment on individual people and practices, but rather it is meant to be a catalyst for shifting our mindset surrounding that trendy topic of "self-care." When we take care of our bodies, we take care of our brains—and vice versa. Perhaps we can also look at the role we play in allowing things like stress to permeate our lives, the lives of our employees, and the lives of our loved ones.

In addition, as you will soon see, there are learning hacks that can enhance our cognitive capacity and even slow the effects of aging on our brains. As we get older, learning may become more difficult, but we can always take actions that help counter the natural decline—and yes, even improve.

10
Learning Hacks

"I am always doing that which I cannot do, in order that I may learn how to do it."

—Pablo Picasso

Earlier in the book, I shared how I had developed *metacognition*, an awareness of my thinking and learning processes, at a young age, opening my mind up to more effective ways to learn new knowledge and skills. For example, one trick you probably already know was associating what I was learning with things I already knew. When I didn't have an association to help aid recall, I would create one by making something up. As another example, in college, I found that I could improve my learning by varying the location of my learning, sometimes intentionally exposing myself to distraction while studying. This idea, which you will see, was supported by research long before I discovered the idea for myself.

We all have the innate capability as humans to develop techniques for learning. It might be a good time for you to pause, close this book, and reflect on those methods and practices you've already uncovered. Recalling these techniques and possibly connecting them to what you will read in this chapter may help cement and strengthen some of your own strategies and deepen your own understanding. You may even develop an insight I haven't covered.

(INTERMISSION)

The learning hacks I'm sharing here have a basis in psychology and neuroscience. These learning hacks, used alone or together, can help you not only learn more effectively and better sustain lifelong learning but may help you expand your learning capability. Learning agility can not only give you a greater edge in your career, but also improve your relationships and provide ongoing fulfillment. Moreover, by embarking on our collective abilities to learn and grow, we are better able to respond to future challenges.

For those of you that like lists to be orderly and MECE (mutually exclusive, collectively exhaustive), get ready to be a little uncomfortable because this list is neither—but hey, it's good for you. You will see that some of these hacks blur into each other. That is OK and can even be helpful because you may do any or all of these things to become a better learner. The inability to categorize these hacks in an orderly way is analogous to the process of learning itself, not neat and methodical, but one that is a little messy and subject to random instances of interference and flashes of momentum.

Learning Hack #1: Learn Hard

Learning is not a spectator sport. You don't learn by being a passive recipient of skills and knowledge. Learning is heightened when we learn in slowly and with discomfort.

Some of us might recall those vintage weight loss belt shakers. I did a quick internet search and found that you can still buy them online. It's hardly surprising, as there is always a market for making difficult things easy, and getting in shape is hard. Just place the band around the fat you want to disappear and turn on the machine while it vibrates away your fat.

In the field of development, I have come across many adult learners who blend learning with entertainment and inspiration. You can be inspired by great presenters and inspiring stories or by seeing people solve complex problems. But learning, and being able to apply that learning to life, means the experience must somehow change our brains. We need to do the hard work of forging new connections in our brain so that we can now solve a math problem, for example, ask for a bottle of wine in French or respond to a partner or colleague with empathy.

When you are a spectator, you risk suffering from the *illusion of competence*, which occurs when you inaccurately perceive that you've learned new knowledge or skills. College students are frequent victims of this illusion when preparing for exams; they think they know the material because it's familiar on the second read of the textbook. On test day, they realize that familiarity is not the same as knowing. The illusion that you are learning and understanding is largely driven by what Professors Elizabeth and Robert Bjork of the Bjork Learning and Forgetting Lab at UCLA called "low-level perceptual priming,"[315] i.e., cues that prime our brain to evoke responses.

I have seen a similar phenomenon in corporate leadership development. Participants can have an *illusion of learning* when an awe-inspiring speaker discusses a topic, such as values-driven leadership, but that doesn't necessarily translate into new behavior. Or participants may understand what excellent leadership communication sounds like. Still, they fail to reflect on their own shortcomings or practice new behaviors and therefore miss opportunities to apply the new ideas to their own communications approaches. Typically, people do not forge new neural connections simply by watching a great presenter—or at least, not nearly as many as do with actual, hands-on learning. I'm not saying keynotes and TED Talks are not helpful—or remarkable, for that matter. These types of presentations often encourage moments of awareness that lead to a reckoning or epiphany that has the potential to change lives. So, we still need inspiring speakers; they're just only the *first* step.

The problem with passive learning is that if you just listen to a story or look at a solution in a book, you haven't embedded those ideas or behaviors into your neural pattern. You are not *changed*. For example, the behavioral change that is required to go from a good leader to a great leader often requires moments of significant discomfort and a pattern of behavior that slowly rewires the brain. As leaders, and often in life, we tend to change most drastically at crucible moments when we realize we are failing or need to do things differently if we want to be successful.

We experience similar illusions when we watch someone else solve a math problem or see a solved equation in the textbook. The steps are shown, and the answer is right there in front of us, and we think: "Of course, that makes sense, so I'm sure I can solve math problems like this." Not only does practice solving a specific type of problem help ensure we know how to solve that type of problem, but practice solving a mix of problem types (called *interleaving*) will help us master the ability to *discern* what strategy to use in solving that type of problem.

Learning is optimized when we take the *slower, more difficult* path to learn.[316] This means working to forge those neural connections through active learning strategies that present "desirable difficulties" and require more time to learn.[317] Next time you need to master something, invest time and effort in these kinds of learning activities:

- Self-assessment or retrieval practice—Take time to recall previously learned knowledge or test yourself on the material. It's one of the most effective ways to cement new knowledge—more effective than re-studying, receiving feedback, or re-reading the material.[318]

- Multiple learning approaches—When learning a new skill, change the way you practice it to master it faster. In a recent study at Johns Hopkins University School of Medicine, participants were asked to learn a computer-based task over the course of two sessions. Those who used a modified learning technique during their second session performed better than those who repeated the same method.

- Interleaving instruction on separate topics or skills— You might recall the volleyball example from Chapter 4. In a blocked practice for volleyball, the players repeat the same skill over and over, like serving, before progressing on to another skill, like setting. In math, blocked practice may mean solving a block of addition problems and then a block of subtraction problems. Interleaving is a "desirable difficulty" that may make the practice seem more difficult but supports learning and remembering.[319] It's also a little more fun to put your practice on shuffle.

- Vary the learning context—Learning, when repeated in the same context, tends to become contextualized.[320] Studies show that recall or skill development can be enhanced if you study in two different rooms rather than one, or if you vary skill practice, like throwing a bean bag at a target at varying distances.[321]

- Space it out—One of the most replicated studies in experimental psychology related to learning is the spacing effect, which reveals that we can better recall knowledge and concepts if we learn them in shorter, multiple, spread-out sessions rather than all at once.[322]

Learning Hack #2: Learn the Thing You Cannot Learn

You don't have to be good at something to learn it. Stretch yourself to boost your neural power, confidence, and resilience.

Many of you have likely heard the quote from Eleanor Roosevelt: "You must do the thing you think you cannot do." The selection is from her book, first published in 1960, *You Learn by Living: Eleven Keys for a More Fulfilling Life.*[323] The context is that you grow stronger when you embrace challenges and difficulties, work through them, and grow confidence and resilience from having endured the challenge.

You might recall the story of the homeschooling mom, from the Introduction, who was "not good at math" and left all the "more difficult" algebra instruction to her engineer husband. Realizing she needed to be a role model to her daughter, she was motivated to learn math and subsequently found she could work through it and learn it. The finding boosted her confidence and resolve in learning math.

Perhaps you see a connection to Bandura's self-efficacy theory here. Recall that self-efficacy is the belief that what you do matters, in other words, the belief that if you put in the effort, it will make a difference. By trying and succeeding, the homeschooling mom boosted her own self-efficacy to master not only math but other difficult subjects as well. Simply the act of plowing through forged new neural pathways and further fortified those pathways that support resilience and courage.

So, learning something difficult results in much more brain activity and development than learning something that is comfortable or that you are good at learning. When you develop a new understanding around difficult and complex subjects, it: 1) forges learning around the topic (just as any other learning activity), and it 2) builds belief in oneself. Moreover, learning difficult subjects helps develop and strengthen neural networks that increase our *capacity to learn* by helping: 3) develop new strategies for more complex learning that leads to the formation of new neural pathways. Furthermore, it 4) strengthens the pathways that enable our ability to power through complex tasks.

An excellent example of the latter phenomenon is when we overcome procrastination to do something we don't want to do. Different neural pathways are triggered when deciding whether to procrastinate depending on whether we see a future value in performing the task. When we are experiencing task-aversiveness, there is an emotional response in the amygdala,[324] fueling a cycle of negative feelings toward a particular task. But if we can see the value of future outcomes of that aversive task and weigh that more heavily, it signals our brain to take a different path, engaging the hippocampus.[325] For example, you may not want to study calculus, but if you consider the future outcome of being a successful engineer, you may overcome your aversiveness to studying calculus.

See the illustration on the next page.

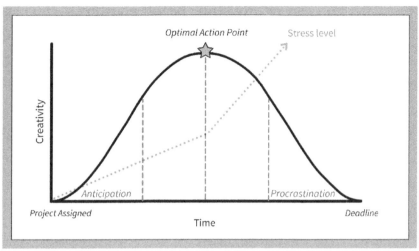

The Sweet Spot: *Habitual procrastinators often feel a surge of motivation when a deadline approaches, while those who compulsively plan ahead feel motivated immediately after being assigned a new task. Regardless, the amygdala's emotional response can cloud the brain's creativity, so taking the hippocampus-based rational approach is optimal.*

Incidentally, repeated procrastination can thicken the neural pathways promoting structural changes in the brain that can make the problem chronic. As many as 20% of all adults suffer from chronic procrastination.[326] In addition to the effects of procrastination, experiencing anxiety around a particular subject has been linked to activating pain networks in the brain.[327]

Research around procrastination has focused on closing the intention-action gap and much of this research is focused on building self-regulatory skills and improving self-efficacy.[328] One way to build these skills and self-efficacy is through practice. In other words, by doing something we don't want to do often enough, we become better at doing things we don't want to do! That makes us better learners, but it also helps us live a fulfilling life in general. Overcoming challenges like procrastination can improve our health and fitness, financial status, and achievement.[329] Mrs. Roosevelt had a point.

An example of learning something challenging and its effect on our brains is learning a second language. Learning a new language can be a powerful tool to increase brain neuroplasticity. In fact, in a study on older adults aged 59-79 years, just four months of language learning increased functional connectivity in the brain's neural language network, which correlated with improvements in global cognitive function.[330]

If the science doesn't motivate you, let me tell you about my daughter. She started taking Spanish classes in high school and wanted to become fluent because she loved the language (and she correctly thought it would look good on her resume). Fast forward to her junior year of college, and she's preparing to study abroad in Ecuador, where she will take all of her classes in Spanish and live with a host family that speaks barely any English. For the first time since she left the house, she's calling me all the time, anxious that she won't be able to succeed because she simply did not believe she had the language skills. Here she was, genuinely believing she could not learn the material, the language, the customs. But faced with no other choice, she learned what she could not learn; she listened, studied, and immersed herself in the experience. She ended up getting a 4.0 that semester. Now, every time she doubts herself, she can recall that experience as proof that she can prove herself wrong.

Take a moment to ask yourself: *what is the thing I cannot learn?* We could all fill a book with things we aren't good at. It could be Photoshop, watercolor, guitar, sewing, coding, physics, or how to make the perfect omelet. Pick one and commit to being 1% better each day. Remind yourself of how your life would improve with that skill, and keep in mind that simply the act of learning it will expand your ability to succeed in every area of your life.

Learning Hack #3: Teach To Learn

To truly understand something, you must be able to explain it to others. Teaching is a powerful form of learning.

As an instructional designer for many years, I've developed a habit of learning by teaching. I had to write and facilitate courses on topics of which I knew very little, and while I relied much on experts, I needed to be able to reshape what I was learning into something that someone else could understand. So much of what I know about professional and leadership skills (and a whole bunch of other topics) is from teaching or at least designing training content.

The expectation that you will need to teach someone else the material you are trying to grasp has been shown to improve memory and recall. In one study conducted at Washington University in St. Louis, Missouri, researchers found that the expectation of teaching changes your mindset. You become more engaged with the material and look for more effective approaches to learning when you anticipate that you will be teaching it to someone rather than simply learning it to pass a test.[331]

A comparable study had a similar outcome in developing or perfecting motor skills.[332] Participants were provided instructions on golf putting and allowed to practice putting. Some study participants were told they would need to teach another person how to putt, while others were told their own performance would be tested. The results revealed that preparing to teach enhanced motor learning, because participants spent more time perfecting their putt if they had to teach it to someone else.[333]

By preparing to teach something—or by imagining you are teaching someone something—you leverage many of the strategies that help you learn. For example, you might actively transform knowledge by relating ideas to previous knowledge or looking for underlying principles and concepts. Moreover, by taking a couple of additional steps to teach someone else your newly acquired skills, you can build additional communication skills as well as boost growth for others.

Learning Hack #4: Stop Thinking So Much

The creative process, and the ability to envision new experiences or concepts, can fuel learning. Reframe your attention, look inward, sleep and dream.

Most of us can relate to having a flash of insight when in the shower, while running, or during some other activity that allows the mind to wander. Often the flash of insight is related to a problem you've been trying to solve, a creative idea, or perhaps just remembering where you left your keys. If you are like me, this act of *spontaneous cognition* will energize you.

In her TEDx Talk, Professor Barbara Oakley of Oakland University contrasts two fundamental modes of thinking: the focused mode and the diffuse mode.[334] According to Oakley, with focused mode, we focus our attention on patterns or movements we already know, like completing a math problem or even learning to play tennis. Most of the time, when we are learning deliberately, we are focusing our attention.[335] I think of focused attention like gazing at a word, a picture, or a flower, noticing the finer details, and being able to describe what you see. This focused mode is also known as *controlled cognition* and refers to deliberately engaging in thought using top-down executive processes.[336]

On the other hand, in what Oakley calls the diffuse mode, we are in daydream mode.[337] In this mode, also known as *spontaneous cognition*, thoughts are relatively free from external and internal constraints, as they are during mind-wandering, night-dreaming, and idea incubation.[338] As an illustration, try this: Find a window if you are indoors and look outside. Focus on something you see, whether it be a tree, a house, or anything. Now, continue to look out your window and, without adjusting your gaze, stop examining whatever you are looking at, and focus your attention inward. You are now in diffuse mode, and this is when spontaneous cognition takes place.

But what is going on inside your brain during spontaneous cognition? When in daydream mode, the human brain is active across a set of cortical brain regions known as the *default network*. Recent neuroscience research characterizes the default network as a set of interacting systems and hubs that play an essential role in "internal mentation"—or the spontaneous, passive state that we all engage in every day when we aren't thinking about anything.[339]

These two key modes of cognitive processing, spontaneous and controlled cognition, focused and diffuse, work together when we are learning a complex skill, such as a language, a musical instrument, or chess. We discern the details in focused mode, then comprehend how everything fits together in diffuse mode.[340] Learning something difficult involves combining creativity and curiosity with execution.

Consider learning to ride a bike. When we only focus on the mechanics of riding a bike, it's fairly difficult. But when we switch modes, from focused to diffuse, we can pull all the pieces together. This effect is most easily observable with physical skills like sports because cognition quickly becomes an obstacle to controlling the body. That's why a coach might tell you when you are learning a skill to stop thinking so much.

What is thought to be happening in the brain is not unlike the role of sleep on learning: the consolidation and re-consolidation of past and present experiences in relation to our current concerns and emotions.[341] A century ago, in 1924, researchers from Cornell pioneered the study of the role of sleep in learning when they noticed discrepancies in Ebbinghaus's Forgetting studies. They tested the rate of forgetting during participants' sleep and awake states and found that memory after sleep was significantly better than after being awake.[342]

Since then, research has placed a heavy emphasis on the role of the REM stage of sleep, which is thought to be involved in the consolidation of procedural memory.[343] Procedural memory is the basis for many motor skills, such as playing the guitar, driving, or skiing. This type of skill is exemplified by a slow learning curve but is very persistent once acquired, hence the phrase, "It's like learning to ride a bike."[344]

It's unclear exactly what happens during sleep and wakefulness, but studies suggest that what occurs is a sort of dialogue between different parts of the brain, where some thoughts are *tagged* for offline replay.[345] Based on my own experience, my theory is that we deliberately tag thoughts that need further solutions. In other words, when we face a conundrum of sorts, we can mark that thought for additional thinking. This may explain why solutions suddenly pop into our head after we stop trying to solve the problem or why sleep seems to help us feel more ready to embark on practicing a recently learned skill.

Whether we are awake and the default network is working or sleeping where an interplay of thoughts occurs, downtime is an important part of learning. I like to think of this unfocused learning as letting thoughts "marinate" while you continue about your daily living. By adding a bit of intention around figuring something out when you are not trying, *you might figure something out when you are not trying.* When faced with a complex problem or ongoing learning endeavor, take a break. Embrace boredom. Zone out for a bit. Sleep on it. And if anyone—including that pesky voice in your head—tries to tell you it's not productive, tell them *it's part of the process.*

Learning Hack #5 Double down on Being Human

Human-only skills are capabilities multipliers. Rather than filling the container of our minds, build a larger container.

The World Economic Forum (WEF) predicted that machines will perform more current work tasks than humans by 2025. That left many of us in corporate learning and development organizations to analyze the implications on the human workforce. One obvious fact remains: humans will still be performing almost 50% of all work tasks. Work performed by humans is still crucial and always will be, but we need to prepare.

The rapid shift over a period of several short years poses urgent challenges to reskill at-risk workers and upskill those whose jobs will evolve. But the question for many employers and workers is around *how* these jobs will evolve.

The paradox of digitization is that technology may either wholly replace jobs or increase them. According to the WEF: "An augmentation strategy takes into account the broader spectrum of value-creating activities that can be accomplished by workers, machines, and algorithms in tandem."[346] Essentially, workers are still needed to do the work that only humans can do.

This means we need to look at what work is to be performed and ask ourselves: what work is primarily human? According to a 2018 report by management consulting firm Kearney, humans on the factory floor continue to contribute most of the value in manufacturing operations. "Machines don't innovate anything," said Doug Neely, a Director of Advanced

Monozukuri Research at Yazaki North America. "Our people are the source of all of our competitiveness. There isn't a machine out there that we could buy that would make us more competitive." [347]

Looking at augmentation scenarios where humans are still needed, we can see clearly: humans solve problems on a spectrum of issues in every industry that machines cannot yet (or perhaps ever) do well. Humans are needed to lend critical thinking and analytical thinking to spot errors and inconsistencies with data models that reinforce bias or make a mistake only humans can notice. Humans are needed to make ethical decisions about the use of gene editing. Humans are needed to empathize, communicate, and collaborate.

In their 2020 Future of Jobs report, the World Economic Forum identified the top 15 skills for 2025:[348]

1	Analytical thinking and innovation
2	Active learning and learning strategies
3	Complex problem-solving
4	Critical thinking and analysis
5	Creativity, originality, and initiative
6	Leadership and social influence
7	Technology use, monitoring, and control
8	Technology design and programming
9	Resilience, stress tolerance, and flexibility
10	Reasoning, problem-solving, and ideation
11	Emotional intelligence
12	Troubleshooting and user experience
13	Service orientation
14	Systems analysis and evaluation
15	Persuasion and negotiation

Top 15 Skills for 2025: Put these on your resume! Companies predict these in-demand skills will be the most crucial in the future workplace.[349]

Most of these fifteen skills, along with perhaps a few others, are what I refer to as *human-only skills* because remarkably, only humans can carry out these skills either in whole or in part (at least for now). They are increasingly relevant in the face of automation and support resilience in the face of change — in this sense, these skills are *durable*. Another common factor among these skills is that they can be leveraged across most disciplines. For example, analytical thinking is helpful in virtually any job, whether you are a brain surgeon, a CEO, a teacher, or a truck driver. Because of this, I consider these skills *portable*.

In addition to being portable and durable, these *human-only skills* are foundational to other skills. One way I like to think of them is that they increase the size of the container of your mind rather than add more knowledge to your existing vessel, an analogy Robert Kegan and Lisa Lahey describe in their book *Immunity to Change*.[350] The analogy means that in being more learning-agile, better at problem-solving, or better as critical thinkers, we make ourselves more capable versus simply acquiring more knowledge. This leads me to the third trait of human-only skills: they are *multiplicative*.

Human-only skills are durable, portable, and multiplicative.

Invest in developing your human-only skills. It will break down the barriers to learning and reinforce your commitment to not just filling your container but also expanding its capacity. It's also critical that we build these skills, and therefore Human

Intelligence (HI), both individually and collectively, as we live into an increasingly complex future.

Where Do You Go from Here?

Hopefully, by the time you've come this far, you have the mindset, the motivation, and the tools to learn. Initially, I intended to include information about the vast array of learning resources available to those who want to continue their learning here. Instead, I've decided to make my resources available more broadly at **hardwiredtolearn.com**. There you will find curated resources to help you on your lifelong learning journey.

The learning resources available to us today compared to a generation ago are like night and day. In addition, as we continue to uncover more evidence about the way we learn, we will no doubt increase our understanding and capability. Nothing is stopping us from becoming lifelong learners. With a commitment to your intention, you can overcome the barriers to learning. And with the tools presented in this book, I encourage you to build a personal infrastructure of learning hacks to keep you on a path of continuous growth and development throughout your life.

Part 5

HI Revolution

11
Prove You Are Human

"If the world is to change for the better, it must start with a change in human consciousness, in the very humanness of modern man."

—Vaclav Havel

Prove you are human. It's something we do every day—sometimes several times a day—when we select the pictures with the crosswalks or click the checkbox to verify, "I'm not a robot."

First used in the early 2000s, challenge-response tests called CAPTCHAs—Completely Automated Public Turing test to tell Computers and Humans Apart—distinguish whether a user is a human or a bot in order to identify and then block malicious activity on websites.[351] The Turing test, originally called the "imitation game" in 1950 by Alan Turing, is a test of a machine's ability to show intelligent behavior that is indistinguishable from that of a human.[352]

Initially patented in 1998, the first CAPTCHAs consisted of letters and numbers sufficiently distorted to prevent recognition by malicious bots, but not so distorted that most humans could not identify the code and retype it.[353] CAPTCHAs serve an important purpose in distinguishing human activity from that of artificial intelligence. Without

CAPTCHAs, mischievous bots can pilfer content to divert ad revenue, commit credit card fraud, launder money, and take over accounts.

The AI-HI Frontier

If you have been paying close attention, you might notice that CAPTCHAs are becoming commonplace and increasingly challenging. Distorted text is progressively more difficult to read, and image-based challenges are fuzzy to the point of being nearly indiscernible. Sometimes you may have to click through multiple rounds of fuzzy images, or you might have to pass various CAPTCHA challenges.

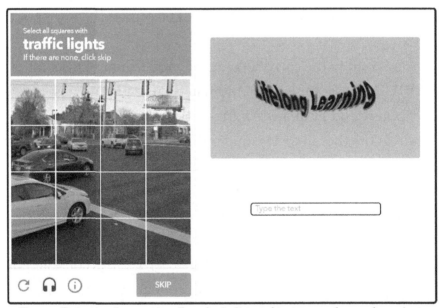

Human-Detection Innovation: From basic distorted text to complex word mosaics to entirely novel forms of challenges, CAPTCHAs have progressed to prove your humanity.

What you may not have noticed is that some CAPTCHAs are becoming increasingly frictionless for the user. On more advanced websites, you might just click a box that says, "I am not a robot." On websites deploying the most sophisticated technology, you may see nothing at all.

What's going on here? Recent advancements in computer vision (CV), AI which seeks to automate human sight, have made automated programs significantly better at solving CAPTCHA challenges. As a result, almost all the traditional CAPTCHA assessments have been broken and have to adapt continually. They adapted initially to become increasingly difficult, in a sort of tit-for-tat in the inevitably losing battle of man versus the machine. If you had been paying attention to media when the machines started catching up, you might have thought this spelled doom for humans.

Since 2014, CAPTCHAs have continued to evolve to meet the growing challenges of AI. *reCAPTCHA*, a tool acquired by Google in 2009, has been evolving to combat the ever-increasing threat of malicious bots while reducing friction for the user.[354] So, for example, in 2014, Google announced the "No CAPTCHA reCAPTCHA."[355] On websites using this application, most users could verify they're human without having to solve a CAPTCHA. Instead, they would just click a checkbox. Invisibly, the application is working on the backend, analyzing the user engagement with the system, to determine whether that user is human.[356]

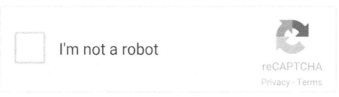

No CAPTCHA reCAPTCHA: This is Google technology.[357]

You might be wondering, *how can humans keep up with the machines?* Perhaps ironically, humans and the machines are working in concert, joining the cybersecurity fight against malicious bots. AI plus HI is being used to combat AI in various cybersecurity applications, including secure application development. According to IBM's website, *Cognitive security with IBM Watson®* leverages the best of both AI and HI, resulting in cybersecurity defenses that get stronger and smarter over time.[358] Chief Technology Officer of IBM Security, Sridhar Muppidi, explains how AI is being used to provide continuous verification that a user is human using *behavioral biometrics,* or patterns of human behavior with an application. Based on those biometrics, the application can subject the user to challenges, such as additional password entry or two-factor authentication, such as texting the user a passphrase. [359]

I think of CAPTCHAs as a metaphor for work that can be accomplished by humans and matched—or multiplied—by machines. Over the last 25 years, we have witnessed an ongoing evolution. Initially, each step forward in HI was met by advances in AI (powered by HI) until the two merged forces and pushed out the frontier of capabilities altogether. So I wonder, *as we consider the future of HI—and the future of work for humans—do we need to explore this frontier more completely and deliberately to examine how we might develop innovative approaches to address the challenges of the modern day? How can we multiply the power of HI through AI?* As we examine our actions, we need to consider how we invest in HI relative to our investment in AI. The Production Possibilities Frontier is a helpful framework for thinking about tradeoffs and investment.

The Production Possibilities Frontier (PPF)

If you took introductory economics, you might remember the concept of the Production Possibilities Frontier (PPF). Essentially, the PPF is a curve that shows the different combinations of the output of two goods that can be produced using available resources. For example, on the following chart, at point A, if you produce 80 units of Good Y, you can produce only 50 units of Good X. At point B, if you produce only Good Y, you forgo the production of Good X; at point C, you produce only Good X.

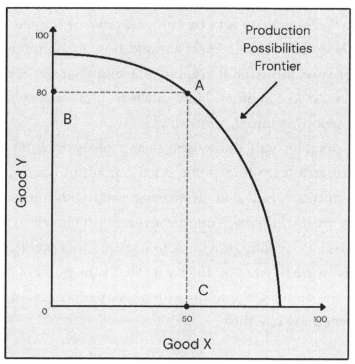

Production Possibilities Frontier: *The production output of good Y is dependent on the production output of Good X, and vice versa. Point A represents a slight prioritization of Good Y over Good X, while Point B and Point C represent a complete lack of production of one good in favor of the other.*

Tradeoffs and Diminishing Returns

At the core of the PPF are the concepts of *tradeoffs* and *diminishing returns*. Producing more of one good means producing less of the other good. Often, when the resources are tax dollars, we think of these tradeoffs as being public goods, such as providing for education versus providing for defense. The PPF offers a range of tough decisions, and the optimal point is never investing all in one or the other.

When I think of diminishing returns, I think of the example from my first Economics 101 teacher. You are at the beach, you are hot and hungry, and you want some ice cream. How much are you willing to pay for one scoop? 2 dollars? Maybe 3? 4? It depends on how hungry you are and how much money you have for sure. But what if you buy one and then someone asks you if you'd like another. How much would you pay for that second scoop? A third? A fourth?

Presumably, you derive increasing pleasure from eating more ice cream up to a point. At the point of continuing to derive pleasure but at a decreasing rate, your pleasure, or returns, are *diminishing*. You may even find yourself at a point where you are wholly unwilling to have another scoop, even if someone were to pay you to buy it. That's the point of *negative return*. The diminishing returns for a scoop of ice cream would look something like this:

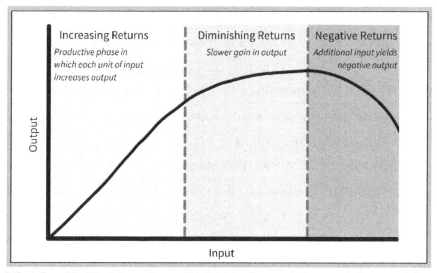

What Goes Up Must Come Down: *Diminishing Returns is the second phase seen below, following increasing returns. For example, the first scoop—and usually the second—of ice cream is quite enjoyable. After that, the pleasure decreases before dropping off altogether (negative returns).*

The AI-HI PPF

Consider the Production Possibilities Frontier again, but this time in the context of funding public education versus defense. You can imagine that if we invest all our resources in defense, eventually, we will experience diminishing returns—i.e., at a certain point, there is increasingly less to gain from increased investment. In addition, there is probably a point at which spending too much on defense could result in negative returns, for example, if we needed to relocate hundreds of millions of people to make room for more military bases or factories. Like any specialized investment, spending more does not guarantee a payoff.

In addition to experiencing diminishing and negative returns, consider the impact on trading education for defense.

Our schools would slowly disappear without funding, causing long-term problems in terms of human capability. The irony is that the enduring impact on human capability would necessarily affect our collective intelligence, and therefore our ability to defend ourselves down the road.

On the other hand, what if we have the best educational system in the world but are threatened by possible attacks from foreign invaders? After all, despite the polarizing nature of these topics, even the most radical politician wouldn't dare propose to cut either program entirely—the U.S. government has consistently funded both entities throughout history. Even the Swiss spend on defense; even the poorest country in the world spends money on both. Optimizing the amount spent on both public goods means considering the diminishing and negative returns of each, as well as the trade-offs of both.

See the illustration on the next page.

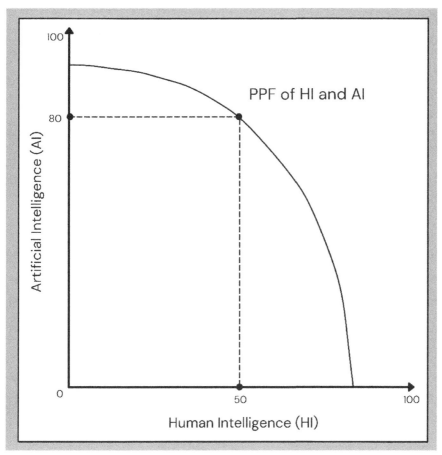

PPF of AI and HI: *There are many complexities behind the PPF of HI and AI, and it is perhaps impossible to know precisely what this curve looks like at any given point. However, by predicting the optimal share of investment in HI and AI, we can maximize our overall returns on humankind's investment in itself.*

Now, think about a Production Possibilities Frontier of AI and HI. Currently, we (companies, governments, schools) are investing in both. But the natural question arises, "Are we optimally investing in HI given our investment in AI?"

Shifting the Curve

While it is useful to consider investing more or less in HI or AI, we can also view the frontier of possibilities itself. What if we could shift the curve outward? Production efficiencies, technology advancements, economic growth, increased investment, and other factors can cause the PPF to shift out. When this happens, the same level of investment brings about greater benefits.

IBM's cognitive security described earlier is an example of a technical advance that shifts out the curve of AI and HI, outwitting the constraints and limitations of the PPF. That is because IBM is combining human intelligence with artificial intelligence, increasing the range of possibilities for both AI and HI.

See the illustration on the next page.

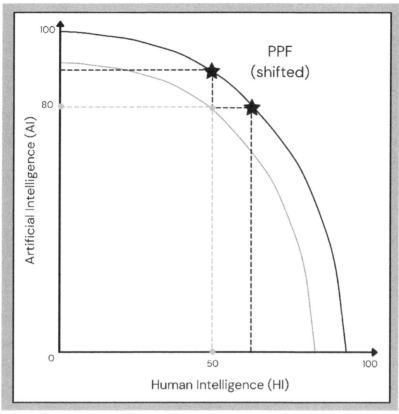

Shifting the Curve: *Technologies like IBM Watson®'s technology combines HI and AI, increasing the returns from investments in both HI and AI, shifting out the curve.*

Throughout history, a convergence of factors has caused many shifts of the PPF, both inward and outward. Technology advancements, mechanization, improved infrastructure, or resource shifts can shift the curve outward. For example, mass production shifted the PPF for various cars and other manufactured goods outward. In the early 1900s, the convergence of mechanized farming equipment, U.S. government incentives, and high wheat and corn prices shifted out the PPF for farmers in the Great Plains. Incidentally, the farmers of those Great Plains states plowed more and more land, disrupting the local ecology. The result was the catastrophic disaster known as the Dust Bowl era, plagued by drought and "dust" storms that were actually displaced topsoil.[360] The PPF, which had expanded over a time of prosperity, contracted quickly, and in so doing displaced tens of thousands of people during another convergence that included the devastating depression in the 1930s.

Pandemics and Paradigm Shifts

In the past, pandemics, colliding with other socio-economic forces and changes, have accelerated massive paradigm shifts, paving the way for growth, progress, and innovation. The COVID-19 pandemic emerged globally in 2020, killing nearly 4.6 million people as of this writing.[361] The pandemic has fueled ongoing uncertainty about the future, disrupting and undermining economies and governments worldwide. As we approach what is hopefully the end of the pandemic, we can begin to see its impacts. According to the Office of the Director of National Intelligence Global Trends 2040 report, the pandemic appears to be accelerating some trends, including deepening inequality, an increasing digital divide, and heightened political polarization. At the same time, improvements in gender equality and widespread reduction in global poverty and disease have reversed.[362]

The Bubonic Plague

Consider the outbreak of the Bubonic Plague in Europe between 1347-1352, which killed more than one-third of

Europe's population and transformed medieval Europe's social and economic systems, causing enormous social disruption. The feudal system collapsed under its own weight as deaths significantly reduced the workforce serving each fiefdom. The number of serfs diminished quickly, and the few survivors could now negotiate for better pay and treatment.[363]

As the population of Europe very slowly recovered, the plague inspired people to rethink the way they were living previously and reconsider their values. This spurred big shifts in socio-economic structures. By the middle of the 15th century, Europe experienced radical changes, including the Protestant Reformation, the agricultural shift from grain farming to animal husbandry, and wage increases for urban and rural laborers.[364]

As the feudal system broke down, and with it the caste system, social mobility became more widespread. People began to shift their mindset from that of a person's "lot in life as a birthright" to that of a person's "merits or abilities transcending one's expectations." This encouraged people to strive on their own and develop their talents to achieve excellence. This brand of individualism was central to the Renaissance and inspired many of the greatest artists, architects, sculptors, and writers.[365]

The Spanish Flu

In the mid-1910s, economists predicted a post-war economic crash as military factory orders dried up after World War I. The "Spanish Flu" outbreak beginning in 1918 heightened the economic uncertainty and instability. Caused by an H1N1 virus with genes of avian origin, influenza killed 50 million people worldwide, more than twice the death toll from World War I.[366] Consider that the death toll from the Spanish Flu was more than ten times higher than the COVID pandemic death toll at the time of this writing,[367] while the global population was less than one-fourth of what it is today, about 1.8 billion in 1918 compared with 7.9 billion in 2021.[368,369]

In the U.S., where the Spanish flu killed 675,000 people and depressed the average life span by ten years, GDP fell by less than 2%. But the decline in economic activity combined with elevated inflation resulted in significant decreases in the real returns on stocks and bonds.[370] After the pandemic, the United States entered a decade of unprecedented growth and prosperity. American consumers, who had patriotically saved during wartime, began to live it up. The "Roaring Twenties" earned its name in history—the U.S. economy grew by 42 percent from 1921 to 1929.[371] Globally, the 1918 pandemic had a broader economic impact. According to researchers, the typical country experienced a reduction of GDP by 6 percent and consumption by 8 percent, declines comparable to those seen in the Great Recession of 2008–2009.[372]

While the economic impacts were mixed, the massive death toll affected how we think about the role of government in healthcare. You could think of the flu as causing a shift in mindset around public health: epidemiology—the study of disease—became legitimized as a science; governments around the world created health ministries; the idea that the highest attainable standard of health is a fundamental right became accepted broadly across the globe.[373] Moreover, the understanding that pandemics are a universal, human problem helped forge an understanding of our own humanity.

An Opportune Moment

While pandemics bring progress, they also hold a mirror to our societies and illuminate relationships with our work, our environment, and with each other. A pandemic reminds us that we are all one species, inextricably linked in our common struggle for survival. A pandemic reminds us that we are human.

Once again, we find ourselves at a convergence of forces that will no doubt usher in yet another new paradigm, but one that we are well-positioned to deliberately shape. 4IR has brought about transformation, and the COVID pandemic has accelerated that change. Increasing digitalization has enabled greater efficiencies than ever before, and this tipping point of digitalization could bring numerous benefits in the form of new prosperity and growth.

Is it possible that it has also accelerated the tipping point of HI? In the corporate sector, there is increasing awareness around building skills—to serve talent redeployment, build digital capability, increase skillsets that complement digitization, and build resilience through interpersonal skills and skills that improve mental health and well-being. An April 2021 McKinsey Global Survey revealed that 69% of company leaders reported an increase in skill-building during the pandemic. Moreover, more than half of those leaders plan to increase their investment in learning in the future.[374]

However, despite the advances brought about by the double disruption of the 4IR and the pandemic, we are witnessing another reality: the double disruption forces have accelerated. This new reality includes growing inequality and widespread poverty, government corruption and political instability, a breakdown of trust in institutions, upside-down labor markets, and ongoing climate change insidiously producing extreme conditions that threaten people's food supply and safety throughout the world. In addition, Dambisa Moyo points to the ongoing problem of lack of global growth, which has been lagging across the globe since the financial collapse of 2008, due in part to what she believes is a lack of long-term thinking about what delivers economic growth at scale. [375]

An Infinite Game

It's difficult to examine these challenges and not hold deep concern about what the future holds. In Chapter 2, I discussed the concept of an *infinite game*, coined by economist James Carse. You might recall that, according to Carse, infinite players see a horizon, a "phenomenon of vision." Every move an infinite player makes is toward that horizon, knowing that they can't reach the horizon but only extend it. [376]

We are all players in an infinite game. Collectively, we have both the agency and the ability to deliberately shape how the next transformation is viewed through the lens of history. Like so many things, it's a matter of intent. When we embrace and adopt our human-only role, we must consider how we are doubling down on our human abilities, abilities that are inherent in all of us through the undeniable and practically limitless ability to learn.

Picking the Learning Card

We have no choice but to learn. So much of what we do already involves learning. As we consider the history of learning and what we know about how we learn, you might recall that we have learned more in the last 20 years than in the previous 200. Could it be that we are at an inflection point where we can leverage all we know about how we learn to catapult human learning into a new era? The promise of AI+HI^2 offers new possibilities; by shifting the AI-HI curve, we can deliberately and successfully address some of the challenges we are experiencing and shape the future paradigm shift.

Through life-long learning, we will all shape the future of HI while benefitting from the many advantages of being a learner. Where digitization illuminates the need to radically accelerate the development of new workforce skills, including higher-order cognitive and technical skills, our ability to address the challenges of today also depends on increased human-only social and emotional skills. This means that not only do we need to develop our abilities to manage and multiply the benefit of the machines, but we also need to expand and develop our abilities to care for each other.

As we think about the future post-COVID, we have an opportunity to craft a future that brings positive progress and transformation. We have a lot to learn and much work to do if we are to be resilient and adapt to our changing world. This represents an opportunity to examine our values, set an intention, and prove we are *genuinely* human.

Acknowledgements

There are people in your career who lift you up and give you a chance. For me, one of these people was Jon Kaplan, now Principal and Founder of Corvantus Consulting and former CLO at Discover. He took a bet on me more than once and helped me recognize I was capable of more than I thought I was. Thanks Jon.

This book would have missed more than one deadline without the help of my amazingly talented daughter, Sage. I am grateful for all her support proofing, footnoting, and illustrating this book as well as single-handedly designing and launching the website. Mark my word, she will do amazing things. Thanks, Boo.

About the Author

Teri Hart is a learning expert and work futurist who has been a leader in learning and development at Fortune 500 and Fortune Global 500 companies in financial services, manufacturing, healthcare, retail industries—having held roles at companies like GE, McKinsey, Discover Financial Services, and Zurich North America.

Teri has personally worked on learning programs affecting tens of thousands of employees throughout her 25+ years of work. She is passionate about life-long learning and its ability to transform who we are.

Teri has a Bachelors in Economics and Political Science from the University of Wisconsin - Milwaukee, a Master's of Science degree in Education from Indiana University, and a Master's in Business Administration from Northwestern University's Kellogg School of Management. She also serves as adjunct faculty at Marquette University.

References

[1] Perlman, A. E. (1962, May 15). *Railroading's Future,* [Excerpt of Speech Transcript]. *Seventy-Five Years of the Econominc Club of Chicago, 82.* https://docplayer.net/64597680-Speeches-transcribed-from-audiocassettes.html

[2] Starbucks Investor Relations. (2020). *Starbucks Reports Q4 Fiscal 2020 Results* [Press Release]. https://investor.starbucks.com/press-releases/financial-releases/press-release-details/2020/Starbucks-Reports-Q4-Fiscal-2020-Results/default.aspx

[3] History.com Editors. (2009, October 29). *Industrial Revolution.* HISTORY. https://www.history.com/topics/industrial-revolution/industrial-revolution

[4] Niller, E. (2019, January 25). *How the Second Industrial Revolution Changed Americans' Lives.* HISTORY. https://www.history.com/news/second-industrial-revolution-advances

[5] Computer History Museum. *Birth of the Computer.* Computerhistory. https://www.computerhistory.org/revolution/birth-of-the-computer/4/78

[6] World Economic Forum. (2020, October 20). *Recession and Automation Changes Our Future of Work, But There are Jobs Coming* [Press Release]. https://www.weforum.org/press/2020/10/recession-and-automation-changes-our-future-of-work-but-there-are-jobs-coming-report-says-52c5162fce

[7] LivePerson. (2021). *About Us.* https://www.liveperson.com/company/

[8] World Economic Forum. (2020, October 20). *Recession and Automation Changes Our Future of Work, But There are Jobs Coming* [Press Release]. https://www.weforum.org/reports/the-future-of-jobs-report-2020

[9] Del Ray, J. (2019, December 11). *How Robots Are Transforming Amazon Warehouse Jobs—for Better and Worse.* Vox. https://www.vox.com/recode/2019/12/11/20982652/robots-amazon-warehouse-jobs-automation

[10] Del Ray, J. (2019, December 11). *How Robots Are Transforming Amazon Warehouse Jobs—for Better and Worse.* Vox. https://www.vox.com/recode/2019/12/11/20982652/robots-amazon-warehouse-jobs-automation

[11] Kldalley6. (2018). Amazon Scout [Photograph]. Wikimedia Commons. https://commons.wikimedia.org/wiki/File:Amazon_Scout.jpg

[12] Amazon.com, Inc. (2019, July 11). *Amazon Pledges to Upskill 100,000 U.S. Employees for In-Demand Jobs by 2025* [Press Release]. https://press.aboutamazon.com/news-releases/news-release-details/amazon-pledges-upskill-100000-us-employees-demand-jobs-2025

[13] Weise, K. (2020, November 27). Pushed by Pandemic, Amazon Goes on a Hiring Spree Without Equal. *The New York Times.* https://www.nytimes.com/2020/11/27/technology/pushed-by-pandemic-amazon-goes-on-a-hiring-spree-without-equal.html

[14] Weise, K. (2020, November 27). Pushed by Pandemic, Amazon Goes on a Hiring Spree Without Equal. *The New York Times.* https://www.nytimes.com/2020/11/27/technology/pushed-by-pandemic-amazon-goes-on-a-hiring-spree-without-equal.html

[15] Weise, K. (2020, November 27). Pushed by Pandemic, Amazon Goes on a Hiring Spree Without Equal. *The New York Times.* https://www.nytimes.com/2020/11/27/technology/pushed-by-pandemic-amazon-goes-on-a-hiring-spree-without-equal.html

[16] Baldwin, R. (2021, January 12). *GM Launches BrightDrop Company to Make Electric Delivery Vehicles.* Car and Driver. https://www.caranddriver.com/news/a35183211/gm-brightdrop-electric-delivery-vehicles-announced/

[17] FleetOwner. (2021, February 5) *Merchants Fleet to Purchase Over 12,600 EV600s from BrightDrop.* https://www.fleetowner.com/fleet-management/press-release/21154331/merchants-fleet-to-purchase-over-12000-ev600s-from-brightdrop

[18] Brain Corp. (2020, July 22). *Brain Corp Surpasses 2 Million Autonomous Hours Powering Largest Fleet of Commercial Mobile Robots in Public Spaces* [Press Release]. https://www.braincorp.com/newsroom/brain-corp-surpasses-2-million-autonomous-hours-powering-largest-fleet-of-commercial-mobile-robots-in-public-spaces/

[19] Day, M. & Gu, J. (2019, March 27). The Enormous Numbers Behind Amazon's Market Reach. *Forbes.* https://www.bloomberg.com/graphics/2019-amazon-reach-across-markets/

[20] Target Corporation. (2021, March 2). *Target Corporation Reports Fourth Quarter and Full-Year 2020 Earnings* [Press Release]. https://corporate.target.com/press/releases/2021/03/target-corporation-reports-fourth-quarter-and-full

[21] Debter, Lauren (2020, May 13). The World's Largest Retailers 2020: Walmart, Amazon Increase Their Lead Ahead of the Pack. *Forbes.* https://www.forbes.com/sites/laurendebter/2020/05/13/the-worlds-largest-retailers-2020-walmart-amazon-increase-lead-ahead-of-the-pack/?sh=488ec15e18d3

[22] McKinsey & Company. (2020, October 5). *How COVID-19 Has Pushed Companies Over the Technology Tipping Point—and Transformed Business Forever.* https://www.mckinsey.com/business-

functions/strategy-and-corporate-finance/our-insights/how-covid-19-has-pushed-companies-over-the-technology-tipping-point-and-transformed-business-forever

[23] Barrero, J. M., Bloom, N., & Davis, S. J. (2020). *COVID-19 Is Also a Reallocation Shock* (Working Paper No. 1010-59). Becker Friedman Institute for Economics at the University of Chicago. https://bfi.uchicago.edu/wp-content/uploads/BFI_WP_202059.pdf

[24] Lund, S. Madgavkar, A., Manyika, J., Smit, S., Ellingrud, K., Robinson, O. (2021, February 18). *The Future of Work After COVID-19*. McKinsey & Company. https://www.mckinsey.com/featured-insights/future-of-work/the-future-of-work-after-covid-19

[25] Schwab, K. (2016 January 14). *The Fourth Industrial Revolution: what it means, how to respond*. World Economic Forum. https://www.weforum.org/agenda/2016/01/the-fourth-industrial-revolution-what-it-means-and-how-to-respond/

[26] New York State Department of Financial Services. (2021). *Report on Apple Card Investigation*. https://cdn.vox-cdn.com/uploads/chorus_asset/file/22392556/rpt_202103_apple_card_investigation.pdf

[27] PwC. (2019). *CEO's curbed confidence spells caution* (22nd Annual Global CEO Survey). https://www.pwc.com/gx/en/ceo-survey/2019/report/pwc-22nd-annual-global-ceo-survey.pdf

[28] von Bartheld, C. S., Bahney, J., & Herculano-Houzel, S. (2016). The search for true numbers of neurons and glial cells in the human brain: A review of 150 years of cell counting. *The Journal of comparative neurology, 524*(18), 3865–3895. https://doi.org/10.1002/cne.24040

[29] World Economic Forum. (2020, October 20). *Recession and Automation Changes Our Future of Work, But There are Jobs Coming* [Press Release]. https://www.weforum.org/reports/the-future-of-jobs-report-2020

[30] Clutch Research. (2020, April 16). 66% of U.S. Employees Are Working Remotely at Least Part-Time During the COVID-19 Pandemic [Press Release]. PRNewswire. https://www.prnewswire.com/news-releases/66-of-us-employees-are-working-remotely-at-least-part-time-during-the-covid-19-pandemic-301041859.html

[31] Hsu, A. (2021, June 24). *As the Pandemic Recedes, Millions of Workers are Saying 'I Quit'*. NPR. https://www.npr.org/2021/06/24/1007914455/as-the-pandemic-recedes-millions-of-workers-are-saying-i-quit

[32] Brown, T. (2017, July 14). *The Gig Economy*. The Daily Beast. https://www.thedailybeast.com/the-gig-economy

[33] U.S. Bureau of Labor Statistics. (2018, June 1). *Independent Contractors made up 6.9 percent of employment in May 2017*.

https://www.bls.gov/opub/ted/2018/independent-contractors-made-up-6-point-9-percent-of-employment-in-may-2017.htm

[34] Kaji, J., Edelman, K., Khan, A., Garia, N., Budman, M., Thomas, R., & Devan, P. (2018). *The rise of the social enterprise: 2018 Deloitte Global Human Capital Trends*. Deloitte Insights. https://www2.deloitte.com/content/dam/insights/us/articles/HCTrends201 8/2018-HCtrends_Rise-of-the-social-enterprise.pdf

[35] Holtz-Eakin, D., Gitis, B., & Rinehart, W. (2017). *The Gig Economy: Research and Policy Implications of Regional, Economic, and Demographic Trends*. The Aspin Institute Future of Work Initiative and American Action Forum . https://www.aspeninstitute.org/wp-content/uploads/2017/02/Regional-and-Industry-Gig-Trends-2017.pdf

[36] Business Roundtable. (2019, August 19). *Business Roundtable Redefines the Purpose of a Corporation to Promote 'An Economy That Serves All Americans'*. https://www.businessroundtable.org/business-roundtable-redefines-the-purpose-of-a-corporation-to-promote-an-economy-that-serves-all-americans

[37] MacMillian, D., Whoriskey, P., & O-Connell, J. (2020, December 16). America's biggest companies are flourishing during the pandemic and putting thousands of people out of work. *The Washington Post*. https://www.washingtonpost.com/graphics/2020/business/50-biggest-companies-coronavirus-layoffs/

[38] Carse, J. P. (2013). *Finite and Infinite Games: A vision of life as play and possibility* (pp. 3). Free Press.

[39] Carse, J. P. (2013). *Finite and Infinite Games: A vision of life as play and possibility* (pp. 62). Free Press.

[40] Sinek, S. (2019). *The Infinite Game* (pp. 4). Portfolio/Penguin.

[41] Fortune. (n.d.). *Fortune 500 2000*. https://fortune.com/fortune500/2000/

[42] Fortune. (n.d.). *Fortune 500 2021*. https://fortune.com/fortune500/2021/

[43] Fortune. (n.d.). *Fortune 500 2000*. https://fortune.com/fortune500/2000/

[44] Fortune. (n.d.). *Fortune 500 2021*. https://fortune.com/fortune500/2021/

[45] Caminiti, S. (2018, March 13). *AT&T's $1 billion gambit: Retraining nearly half its workforce for jobs of the future*. CNBC. https://www.cnbc.com/2018/03/13/atts-1-billion-gambit-retraining-nearly-half-its-workforce.html

[46] Caminiti, S. (2018, March 13). *AT&T's $1 billion gambit: Retraining nearly half its workforce for jobs of the future*. CNBC. https://www.cnbc.com/2018/03/13/atts-1-billion-gambit-retraining-nearly-half-its-workforce.html

[47] McDonald's Corporation. (2018, March 29). *McDonald's Triples Crew Tuition Assistance for Restaurant Employees, Lowers Eligibility*

Requirements to 90 Days [Press Release].
https://corporate.mcdonalds.com/corpmcd/en-us/our-stories/article/ourstories.triples_crew_tuition.html

[48] Prokopeak, M. (2019, July 11). *Amazon Goes Big With $700 Million Reskilling Pledge.* Chief Learning Officer. https://www.chieflearningofficer.com/2019/07/11/amazon-goes-big-with-700-million-reskilling-pledge/

[49] Cutter, C. (2020, December 10). Amazon Wants to Train 29 Million People to Work in the Cloud. *The Wall Street Journal.* https://www.wsj.com/articles/amazon-wants-to-train-29-million-people-to-work-in-the-cloud-11607621622

[50] Walmart. (2021, July 27). Walmart To Pay 100% of College Tuition and Books for Associates [Press release]. https://corporate.walmart.com/newsroom/2021/07/27/walmart-to-pay-100-of-college-tuition-and-books-for-associates

[51] Target. (2021, Aug 4) Target Launching Debt-Free Education Assistance Program to More Than 340,000 Frontline Team Members [Press release]. https://corporate.target.com/press/releases/2021/08/Target-Launching-Debt-Free-Education-Assistance-Pr

[52] Guild Education. https://www.guildeducation.com/

[53] Lau, Y. (2020, January 6). *How (and Why) Companies Should Engage the Liquid Workforce.* Forbes. https://www.forbes.com/sites/forbeshumanresourcescouncil/2020/01/06/how-and-why-companies-should-engage-the-liquid-workforce/?sh=1f1e91a6f927

[54] Difference Between Fluid and Liquid [Online Course]. Vendantu. https://www.vedantu.com/chemistry/difference-between-fluid-and-liquid

[55] HolacracyOne, LLC. https://www.holacracy.org

[56] Bersin, Josh. (2020, July 18). Talent Marketplace Performs Explode Into View. https://joshbersin.com/2020/07/talent-marketplace-platforms-explode-into-view/

[57] Unilever, (2019, June 24). *Unilever launches new AI-powered talent marketplace* [Press Release]. https://www.unilever.com/news/press-releases/2019/unilever-launches-ai-powered-talent-marketplace.html

[58] Fink, L. (2021). *Larry Fink's 2021 Letter to CEOs.* BlackRock.. https://www.blackrock.com/corporate/investor-relations/larry-fink-ceo-letter

[59] Fink, L. (2021). Larry Fink's 2021 Letter to CEOs. BlackRock.. https://www.blackrock.com/corporate/investor-relations/larry-fink-ceo-letter

[60] Zahidi, S., Ratcheva, V., Hingel, G., & Brown, S. (2020). *The Future of Jobs Report*. World Economic Forum. http://www3.weforum.org/docs/WEF_Future_of_Jobs_2020.pdf

[61] Collins, J. (2001). *Good to Great: Why Some Companies Make the Leap and Others Don't* (pp. 83-86). HarperBusiness.

[62] National Research Council. (2000). *How People Learn: Brain, Mind, Experience, and School: Expanded Edition*. The National Academies Press. https://doi.org/10.17226/9853

[63] Lents, N. H. (2018, March 26). *In Humans and Animals, Social Learning Drives Intelligence*. Psychology Today. https://www.psychologytoday.com/us/blog/beastly-behavior/201803/in-humans-and-animals-social-learning-drives-intelligence

[64] UC San Diego School of Medicine. (n.d.). *What is fMRI?*. Retrieved August 8, 2021, from http://fmri.ucsd.edu/Research/whatisfmri.html

[65] Seel, N.M. (2012). *History of the Sciences of Learning*. Encyclopedia of the Sciences of Learning. Springer. https://doi.org/10.1007/978-1-4419-1428-6_916

[66] Steup, M. & Ram, N. (2020). Epistemology. *The Stanford Encyclopedia of Philosophy* (Fall 2020 Edition). https://plato.stanford.edu/archives/fall2020/entries/epistemology/

[67] Steup, M. & Ram, N. (2020). Epistemology. *The Stanford Encyclopedia of Philosophy* (Fall 2020 Edition). https://plato.stanford.edu/archives/fall2020/entries/epistemology/

[68] Hansing, O. (1928). The Doctrine of Recollection in Plato's Dialogues. *The Monist, 38*(2), 231-262. http://www.jstor.org/stable/27901150

[69] Burnet, J. (1967). *Aristotle on Education*. Cambridge University Press. https://www.amazon.com/Aristotle-Education-Extracts-Ethics-Politics/dp/0521094437

[70] Martinich, A. & Stroll, A. (2021, February 11). *Epistemology: St. Thomas Aquinas*. Encyclopedia Britannica. https://www.britannica.com/topic/epistemology/Scientific-theology-to-secular-science

[71] Hatfield, G. (2018). René Descartes. *The Stanford Encyclopedia of Philosophy* (Summer 2018 Edition). https://plato.stanford.edu/archives/sum2018/entries/descartes/

[72] Hatfield, G. (2018). René Descartes. *The Stanford Encyclopedia of Philosophy* (Summer 2018 Edition). https://plato.stanford.edu/archives/sum2018/entries/descartes/

[73] Hatfield, G. (2018). René Descartes. *The Stanford Encyclopedia of Philosophy* (Summer 2018 Edition). https://plato.stanford.edu/archives/sum2018/entries/descartes/

[74] Rogers, G. (2021, January 13). *John Locke*. Encyclopedia Britannica. https://www.britannica.com/biography/John-Locke

[75] Rogers, G. (2021, January 13). *John Locke*. Encyclopedia Britannica. https://www.britannica.com/biography/John-Locke

[76] Nakosteen, M., Scanlon, D., Arnove,R., Vázquez, J., Anweiler, O., Chen, T., Thomas, R., Marrou, H., Bowen, J. , Gelpi, E., Lauwerys, J., Meyer, A., Riché, P., Ipfling, H., Lawson, R., Szyliowicz, J., Swink, R., Mehdi, K., Chambliss, J.J., ... Mukerji, S.N. (2021, May 1). *Western Education in the 19ᵗʰ Century*. Encyclopedia Britannica. https://www.britannica.com/topic/education/Western-education-in-the-19th-century

[77] Ebbinghaus, H. (2013). Memory: A contribution to Experimental Psychology (H. A. Ruger & C. E. Bussenius, Trans.). *Annals of Neurosciences, 20*(4), 155-156. (1913). https://doi.org/10.5214/ans.0972.7531.200408

[78] Ivie, S. (2006). The Legacy of William James. *Journal of Thought, 41*(4), 117-136. http://www.jstor.org/stable/42589899

[79] Ivie, S. (2006). The Legacy of William James. *Journal of Thought, 41*(4), 117-136. http://www.jstor.org/stable/42589899

[80] McSweeney, F. K., & Murphy, E. S. (2014). Part I: Basic Classical Conditioning. In *The Wiley Blackwell Handbook of Operant and Classical Conditioning* (pp. 44-145). John Wiley & Sons, Inc.

[81] Thorndike, E. L. (1927). The law of effect. *The American Journal of Psychology, 39*, 212–222. https://doi.org/10.2307/1415413

[82] McSweeney, F. K., & Murphy, E. S. (2014). Part III: Basic Operant Conditioning. In *The Wiley Blackwell Handbook of Operant and Classical Conditioning* (pp. 221-530). John Wiley & Sons, Inc.

[83] Western Governors University. (2020, May 29). *What is the Behavioral Learning Theory?* https://www.wgu.edu/blog/what-behavioral-learning-theory2005.html

[84] Snelbecker, G. E. (1987). Contrasting and Complementary Approaches to Instructional Design. In C.M. Reigeluth (Ed.), *Instructional Theories in Action* (pp. 321-337). Routledge Publishing. https://doi.org/10.4324/9780203056783

[85] Ojose, B. (2008). Applying Piaget's Theory of Cognitive Development to Mathematics Instruction. *The Mathematics Educator, 18*(1), 26-30. https://files.eric.ed.gov/fulltext/EJ841568.pdf

[86] Ojose, B. (2008). Applying Piaget's Theory of Cognitive Development to Mathematics Instruction. *The Mathematics Educator, 18*(1), 26-30. https://files.eric.ed.gov/fulltext/EJ841568.pdf

[87] Piaget, Jean. (1952). *The Origin of Intelligence in Children* (pp. 220) (M. Cook, Trans.). International Universities Press. (Original work published 1936) https://www.pitt.edu/~strauss/origins_r.pdf

[88] Piaget, Jean. (1952). *The Origin of Intelligence in Children* (pp. 220) (M. Cook, Trans.). International Universities Press. (Original work published 1936) https://www.pitt.edu/~strauss/origins_r.pdf pp. 185

[89] Takaya, K. (2008). Jerome Bruner's Theory of Education: From Early Bruner to Later Bruner. *Interchange, 39*, 1–19. https://doi.org/10.1007/s10780-008-9039-2

[90] Takaya, K. (2008). Jerome Bruner's Theory of Education: From Early Bruner to Later Bruner. *Interchange, 39*, 1–19. https://doi.org/10.1007/s10780-008-9039-2

[91] Simon, H.A. (1996). *The Sciences of the Artificial* (3rd Ed.) (p. 92). MIT Press.

[92] La Berge, A.F. (2008). How the Ideology of Low-Fat Conquered America. *Journal of the History of Medicine and Allied Sciences, 63*(2), 139-177. https://doi.org/10.1093/jhmas/jrn001

[93] La Berge, A.F. (2008). How the Ideology of Low-Fat Conquered America. *Journal of the History of Medicine and Allied Sciences, 63*(2), 139-177. https://doi.org/10.1093/jhmas/jrn001

[94] La Berge, A.F. (2008). How the Ideology of Low-Fat Conquered America. *Journal of the History of Medicine and Allied Sciences, 63*(2), 139-177. https://doi.org/10.1093/jhmas/jrn001

[95] La Berge, A.F. (2008). How the Ideology of Low-Fat Conquered America. *Journal of the History of Medicine and Allied Sciences, 63*(2), 139-177. https://doi.org/10.1093/jhmas/jrn001

[96] La Berge, A.F. (2008). How the Ideology of Low-Fat Conquered America. *Journal of the History of Medicine and Allied Sciences, 63*(2), 139-177. https://doi.org/10.1093/jhmas/jrn001

[97] Centers for Disease Control and Prevention. (1999, October 26). *Obesity epidemic increases dramatically in the United States: CDC director calls for national prevention effort* [Press release]. https://www.cdc.gov/media/pressrel/r991026.htm

[98] Taubes, G. (2002, July 7). What if it's all been a lie? *The New York Times Magazine.* https://www.nytimes.com/2002/07/07/magazine/what-if-it-s-all-been-a-big-fat-lie.html

[99] Santos, F. L., Esteves, S.S., da Costa Pereira, A., Yancy, W. S., & Nunes, J. P. L. (2012). Systematic review and meta-analysis of clinical trials of the effects of low carbohydrate diets on cardiovascular risk factors. *Obesity Reviews, 13*(11), 1048-1066. https://doi.org/10.1111/j.1467-789X.2012.01021.x

[100] Samaha, F. F., Iqbal, N., Seshadri, P., Chicano, K. L., Daily, D. A., McGrory, J., Williams, T., Williams, M., Gracely, E. J., & Stern, L. (2003). A Low-Carbohydrate as Compared with a Low-Fat Diet in Severe Obesity. *The New England Journal of Medicine, 348*, 2074-2081. https://doi.org/10.1056/NEJMoa022637

[101] Wansink, B., & Chandon, P. (2006). Can "Low-Fat" Nutrition Labels Lead to Obesity? *Journal of Marketing Research, 43*(4), 605–617. https://doi.org/10.1509/jmkr.43.4.605

[102] Bisquick Original Pancake Mix. (n.d.). Betty Crocker. https://www.bettycrocker.com/products/bisquick/bisquick-original

[103] Bisquick Heart Healthy Pancake Mix. (n.d.). Betty Crocker. https://www.bettycrocker.com/products/bisquick/bisquick-heart-smart-pancake-and-baking-mix

[104] McGuire Woods. (2013, November 4.) https://www.mcguirewoods.com/client-resources/Alerts/2013/11/Heart-Healthy-Redefined

[105] Trading Places. (2021, July 9). In *Wikipedia.* https://en.wikipedia.org/w/index.php?title=Trading_Places&oldid=1032830506

[106] Noble, K. (2019, January 24). *How does income affect childhood brain development?* [Video]. TED Salon. https://www.ted.com/talks/kimberly_noble_how_does_income_affect_childhood_brain_development/transcript?language=en

[107] Ramachandran, V.S. (2002). Encyclopedia of the human brain. Academic Press. https://www.sciencedirect.com/referencework/9780122272103/encyclopedia-of-the-human-brain#book-info

[108] Noble, K. (2019, January 24). *How does income affect childhood brain development?* [Video]. TED Salon. https://www.ted.com/talks/kimberly_noble_how_does_income_affect_childhood_brain_development/transcript?language=en

[109] Buchaniec, C. (2019, April 4). *The wealthy have always had the academic advantage.* The Daily Northwestern. https://dailynorthwestern.com/2019/04/04/opinion/buchaniec-the-wealthy-have-always-had-the-academic-advantage/

[110] Steele, C., & Aronson, J. (1995). Stereotype threat and the intellectual test performance of African Americans. *Journal of Personality and Social Psychology*, 69(5), 797–811. https://doi.org/10.1037/0022-3514.69.5.797

[111] Steele, C., & Aronson, J. (1995). Stereotype threat and the intellectual test performance of African Americans. *Journal of Personality and Social Psychology*, 69(5), 797–811. https://doi.org/10.1037/0022-3514.69.5.797

[112] McElroy, M. (2011, March 14). *Gender stereotypes about math develop as early as second grade.* Washington University News. https://www.washington.edu/news/2011/03/14/gender-stereotypes-about-math-develop-as-early-as-second-grade/

[113] Noble, K. (2019, January 24). *How does income affect childhood brain development?* [Video]. TED Salon. https://www.ted.com/talks/kimberly_noble_how_does_income_affect_childhood_brain_development/transcript?language=en

[114] Noble, K. (2019, January 24). *How does income affect childhood brain development?* [Video]. TED Salon. https://www.ted.com/talks/kimberly_noble_how_does_income_affect_childho od_brain_development/transcript?language=en

[115] Konkel, L. (2018, November 20). The Brain Before Birth: Using fMRI to Explore the Secrets of Fetal Neurodevelopment. *Environmental Health Perspectives, 126*(11). https://doi.org/10.1289/EHP2268

[116] Dweck, C. S. (2007). *Mindset: The New Psychology of Success,* pp. 7-10. Ballantine Books.

[117] Dweck, C. S. (2007). *Mindset: The New Psychology of Success,* pp. 7-10. Ballantine Books.

[118] Aronson, J., Fried, C. B., & Good, C. (2002*).* Reducing the Effects of Stereotype Threat on African American College Students by Shaping Theories of Intelligence. *Journal of Experimental Social Psychology, 38*(2), 113-125. https://doi.org/10.1006/jesp.2001.1491

[119] Aronson, J., Fried, C. B., & Good, C. (2002*).* Reducing the Effects of Stereotype Threat on African American College Students by Shaping Theories of Intelligence. *Journal of Experimental Social Psychology, 38*(2), 113-125. https://doi.org/10.1006/jesp.2001.1491

[120] Gardner, H. (1983). *Frames of Mind: The Theory of Multiple Intelligences.* Basic Books.

[121] Gardner, H. (1983). *Frames of Mind: The Theory of Multiple Intelligences.* Basic Books.

[122] Strauss, V. (2013, October 16). Howard Gardner: 'Multiple intelligences' are not 'learning styles'. *The Washington Post.* https://www.washingtonpost.com/news/answer-sheet/wp/2013/10/16/howard-gardner-multiple-intelligences-are-not-learning-styles/

[123] Khazan, O. (2018, April 11). *The Myth of 'Learning Styles'.* The Atlantic. https://www.theatlantic.com/science/archive/2018/04/the-myth-of-learning-styles/557687/

[124] Khazan, O. (2018, April 11). *The Myth of 'Learning Styles'.* The Atlantic. https://www.theatlantic.com/science/archive/2018/04/the-myth-of-learning-styles/557687/

[125] Alvarez-Montero, F. J., Leyva-Cruz, M. G., & Moreno-Alcaraz, F. (2018). Learning Styles Inventories: an update of Coffield, Moseley, Hall, & Ecclestone's Reliability and Validity Matrix. *Journal of Research in Educational Psychology, 16*(46), 597-629. https://doi.org/10.25115/ejrep.v16i46.2237

[126] Pashler, H., Mcdaniel, M., Rohrer, D., & Bjork, R. (2009). Learning Styles: Concepts and Evidence. *Psychological Science in the Public Interest, 9*(3), 105-119. https://doi.org/10.1111/j.1539-6053.2009.01038.x

[127] Knoll, A.R., Otani, H., Skeel, R.L., Van Horn, K.R. (2017). Learning style, judgements of learning, and learning of verbal and visual information. *British Journal of Psychology, 108*(3) 544-563. https://doi.org/10.1111/bjop.12214

[128] Husmann, P.R., & O'Loughlin, V.D. (2018). Another Nail in the Coffin for Learning Styles? Disparities among Undergraduate Anatomy Students' Study Strategies, Class Performance, and Reported VARK Learning Styles. *Anatomical Sciences Education, 12*(1), 6-19. https://doi.org/10.1002/ase.1777

[129] Khazan, O. (2018, April 11). *The Myth of 'Learning Styles'*. The Atlantic. https://www.theatlantic.com/science/archive/2018/04/the-myth-of-learning-styles/557687/

[130] Duckworth, Angela (2018). *Grit: The Power of Passion and Perseverance*. Scribner.

[131] Duckworth, Angela (2018). *Grit: The Power of Passion and Perseverance*. Scribner. p. 15.

[132] STACK. (2018, August 20). *3 Effective, Fun Volleyball Serving Drills*. https://www.stack.com/a/volleyball-serving-drills/

[133] Koriat, A., & Bjork, R. A. (2005). Illusions of Competence in Monitoring One's Knowledge During Study. *Journal of Experimental Psychology: Learning, Memory, and Cognition, 31*(2), 187-194. https://doi.org/10.1037/0278-7393.31.2.187

[134] Phaidon. (n.d.). *How, After Death, Hokusai Changed art History*. Retrieved July 29, 2021, from https://www.phaidon.com/agenda/art/articles/2017/may/10/how-after-death-hokusai-changed-art-history/

[135] Smith, H. D. (1988). *Hokusai: One Hundred Views of Mt. Fuji*. George Braziller.

[136] The Julia Child Foundation for Gastronomy and the Culinary Arts. https://juliachildfoundation.org

[137] The Julia Child Foundation for Gastronomy and the Culinary Arts. https://juliachildfoundation.org

[138] Armour, K. (2013, April 15). *Top 20 Julia Child Quotes*. Matchbook. https://www.matchbookmag.com/daily/47-top-20-julia-child-quotes

[139] Gage, F. H. (2004). Structural plasticity of the adult brain. *Dialogues in clinical neuroscience, 6*(2), 135–141. https://doi.org/10.31887/DCNS.2004.6.2/fgage

[140] Gilbert, Daniel (2014). *The Psychology of Your Future Self* [Video]. TED. https://www.ted.com/talks/dan_gilbert_the_psychology_of_your_future_self?language=en

[141] Quiodbach, J., Gilbert, D. T., & Wilson, T. D. (2013). The End of History Illusion. *Science, 339*(5115), 96-98. https://doi.org/10.1126/science.1229294

[142] Quiodbach, J., Gilbert, D. T., & Wilson, T. D. (2013). The End of History Illusion. Science, 339(5115), 96-98. https://doi.org/10.1126/science.1229294

[143] Colucci-D'Amato, L., Bonavita, V., & di Porzio, U. (2006). The end of the central dogma of neurobiology: stem cells and neurogenesis in adult CNS.

Neurological Sciences: Official Journal of the Italian Neurological Society and of the Italian Society of Clinical Neurophysiology, 27(4), 266–270. https://doi.org/10.1007/s10072-006-0682-z

[144] Colucci-D'Amato, L., Bonavita, V., & di Porzio, U. (2006). The end of the central dogma of neurobiology: stem cells and neurogenesis in adult CNS. *Neurological Sciences: Official Journal of the Italian Neurological Society and of the Italian Society of Clinical Neurophysiology, 27*(4), 266–270. https://doi.org/10.1007/s10072-006-0682-z

[145] Wongupparaj, P., Kumari, V., & Morris, R. G. (2015). A Cross-Temporal Meta-Analysis of Raven's Progressive Matrices: Age groups and developing versus developed countries. Intelligence, 49, 1-9. https://doi.org/10.1016/j.intell.2014.11.008

[146] Flynn, J. R. (2012). Are We Getting Smarter?: Rising IQ in the Twenty-First Century. Cambridge University Press.

[147] von Bartheld, C. S., Bahney, J., & Herculano-Houzel, S. (2016). The search for true numbers of neurons and glial cells in the human brain: A review of 150 years of cell counting. *The Journal of comparative neurology, 524*(18), 3865–3895. https://doi.org/10.1002/cne.24040

[148] Dance, A. (2020, November 18). *Making and Breaking Connections in the Brain.* BrainFacts. https://www.brainfacts.org/brain-anatomy-and-function/cells-and-circuits/2020/making-and-breaking-connections-in-the-brain-111820

[149] Karabanov, A., & Ullen, F. (2008). Implicit and Explicit Learning of Temporal Sequences Studied with the Process Dissociation Procedure. Journal of Neurophysiology, 100(2), 733-739. https://doi.org/10.1152/jn.01303.2007

[150] Keysers, C., & Gazzola, V. (2014). Hebbian learning and predictive mirror neurons for actions, sensations and emotions. *Philosophical transactions of the Royal Society of London B, 369*(1644), 20130175. https://doi.org/10.1098/rstb.2013.0175

[151] Keysers, C., & Gazzola, V. (2014). Hebbian learning and predictive mirror neurons for actions, sensations and emotions. *Philosophical transactions of the Royal Society of London B, 369*(1644), 20130175. https://doi.org/10.1098/rstb.2013.0175

[152] Keysers, C., & Gazzola, V. (2014). Hebbian learning and predictive mirror neurons for actions, sensations and emotions. *Philosophical transactions of the Royal Society of London B, 369*(1644), 20130175. https://doi.org/10.1098/rstb.2013.0175

[153] Kandel, E.R. (2001, Dec). The Molecular Biology of Memory Storage: A Dialog between Genes and Synapses. In Nobel Symposia (Lecture). Lecture conducted in Stockholm, Sweden. Eric R. Kandel—Nobel Symposia (nobelprize.org)

[154] Kandel, E.R. (2001, Dec). The Molecular Biology of Memory Storage: A Dialog between Genes and Synapses. In Nobel Symposia (Lecture). Lecture

conducted at Karolinska Institutet, Stockholm, Sweden. Eric R. Kandel—Nobel Symposia (nobelprize.org)

[155] Kandel, E.R. (2001, Dec). The Molecular Biology of Memory Storage: A Dialog between Genes and Synapses. In Nobel Symposia (Lecture). Lecture conducted in Stockholm, Sweden. Eric R. Kandel—Nobel Symposia (nobelprize.org)

[156] Kandel, E.R. (2001, Dec). The Molecular Biology of Memory Storage: A Dialog between Genes and Synapses. In Nobel Symposia (Lecture). Lecture conducted in Stockholm, Sweden. Eric R. Kandel—Nobel Symposia (nobelprize.org)

[157] Kandel, E.R. (2001, Dec). The Molecular Biology of Memory Storage: A Dialog between Genes and Synapses. In Nobel Symposia (Lecture). Lecture conducted in Stockholm, Sweden. Eric R. Kandel—Nobel Symposia (nobelprize.org)

[158] Arizona State University. (2019, March 6). *More than just memories: A new role for the hippocampus during learning.* ScienceDaily. www.sciencedaily.com/releases/2019/03/190306081704.htm

[159] Arizona State University. (2019, March 6). *More than just memories: A new role for the hippocampus during learning.* ScienceDaily. www.sciencedaily.com/releases/2019/03/190306081704.htm

[160] Maguire, E. A., Gadian, D. G., Johnsrude, I. S., Good, C. D., Ashburner, J., Frackowiak, R. S., Frith, C. D. (2000). Navigation-related structural change in the hippocampi of taxi drivers. *Proceedings of the National Academy of Sciences, 97*(8), 4398-4403. https://doi.org/10.1073/pnas.070039597

[161] Maguire, E. A., Gadian, D. G., Johnsrude, I. S., Good, C. D., Ashburner, J., Frackowiak, R. S., Frith, C. D. (2000). Navigation-related structural change in the hippocampi of taxi drivers. *Proceedings of the National Academy of Sciences, 97*(8), 4398-4403. https://doi.org/10.1073/pnas.070039597

[162] Maguire, E. A., Gadian, D. G., Johnsrude, I. S., Good, C. D., Ashburner, J., Frackowiak, R. S., Frith, C. D. (2000). Navigation-related structural change in the hippocampi of taxi drivers. *Proceedings of the National Academy of Sciences, 97*(8), 4398-4403. https://doi.org/10.1073/pnas.070039597

[163] McKetton, L., DeSimone, K., & Schneider, K. A. (2019). Larger Auditory Cortical Area and Broader Frequency Tuning Underlie Absolute Pitch. *The Journal of Neuroscience, 39*(15), 2930–2937. https://doi.org/10.1523/JNEUROSCI.1532-18.2019

[164] Fields, D. R. (2020). The Brain Learns in Unexpected Ways. *Scientific American, 322*(3), 74-79. https://www.scientificamerican.com/article/the-brain-learns-in-unexpected-ways/

[165] Fields, D. R. (2020). The Brain Learns in Unexpected Ways. *Scientific American, 322*(3), 74-79. https://www.scientificamerican.com/article/the-brain-learns-in-unexpected-ways/

[166] Voss, P., Thomas, M. E., Cisneros-Franco, J. M., & de Villers-Sidani, É. (2017). Dynamic Brains and the Changing Rules of Neuroplasticity: Implications for Learning and Recovery. *Frontiers in Psychology, 8*, 1657. https://doi.org/10.3389/fpsyg.2017.01657

[167] Berlucchi, G., & Buchtel, H. A. (2009). Neuronal plasticity: historical roots and evolution of meaning. *Experimental brain research, 192*(3), 307–319. https://doi.org/10.1007/s00221-008-1611-6

[168] Liou, S. (2010, June 26). *Neuroplasticity.* Huntington's Outreach Project for Education at Stanford (HOPES). https://hopes.stanford.edu/neuroplasticity/#strategies-for-promoting-brain-reorganization

[169] Cheng, A., Hou, Y., & Mattson, M. P. (2010). *Mitochondria and neuroplasticity.* ASN neuro, 2(5), e00045. https://doi.org/10.1042/AN20100019

[170] Su, Y. S., Veeravagu, A., & Grant, G. (2016) Neuroplasticity after Traumatic Brain Injury. In D. Laskowitz & G. Grant (Eds.), *Translational Research in Traumatic Brain Injury* (Chapter 8). CRC Press/Taylor and Francis Group. https://www.ncbi.nlm.nih.gov/books/NBK326735/

[171] Liou, S. (2010, June 26). *Neuroplasticity.* Huntington's Outreach Project for Education at Stanford (HOPES). https://hopes.stanford.edu/neuroplasticity/#strategies-for-promoting-brain-reorganization

[172] Hochman, D. (2020, January 30). *Harvard Researcher's 8-Year Quest to Regain Her Health After a Massive Stroke.* AARP. https://www.aarp.org/entertainment/celebrities/info-2020/jill-bolte-taylor.html

[173] Deng, W., Aimone, J. & Gage, F. (2010). New neurons and new memories: How does adult hippocampal neurogenesis affect learning and memory? *Nature Reviews Neuroscience, 11*, 339–350. https://doi.org/10.1038/nrn2822

[174] Deng, W., Aimone, J. & Gage, F. (2010). New neurons and new memories: How does adult hippocampal neurogenesis affect learning and memory? *Nature Reviews Neuroscience, 11*, 339–350. https://doi.org/10.1038/nrn2822

[175] Danner, D. D., Snowdon, D. A., & Friesen, W. V. (2000). Positive Emotions in Early Life and Longevity: Findings from the Nun Study. *Journal of Personality and Social Psychology, 80*(5), 804-813. https://doi.org/10.1037/0022-3514.80.5.804

[176] Danner, D. D., Snowdon, D. A., & Friesen, W. V. (2000). Positive Emotions in Early Life and Longevity: Findings from the Nun Study. *Journal of Personality and Social Psychology, 80*(5), 804-813. https://doi.org/10.1037/0022-3514.80.5.804

[177] Danner, D. D., Snowdon, D. A., & Friesen, W. V. (2000). Positive Emotions in Early Life and Longevity: Findings from the Nun Study. *Journal of Personality and Social Psychology, 80*(5), 804-813. https://doi.org/10.1037/0022-3514.80.5.804

[178] Danner, D. D., Snowdon, D. A., & Friesen, W. V. (2000). Positive Emotions in Early Life and Longevity: Findings from the Nun Study. *Journal of Personality and Social Psychology, 80*(5), 804-813. https://doi.org/10.1037/0022-3514.80.5.804

[179] Raz, G (Host). (2017, July 21). Lisa Genova: Can Alzheimer's Disease Be Prevented? [Interview Transcript]. NPR. https://www.npr.org/transcripts/537016132

[180] Raz, G (Host). (2017, July 21). Lisa Genova: Can Alzheimer's Disease Be Prevented? [Interview Transcript]. NPR. https://www.npr.org/transcripts/537016132

[181] Raz, G (Host). (2017, July 21). Lisa Genova: Can Alzheimer's Disease Be Prevented? [Interview Transcript]. NPR. https://www.npr.org/transcripts/537016132

[182] Stanford University Medical Center. (2010, November 17). *Stunning Details of Brain Connections Revealed.* ScienceDaily. www.sciencedaily.com/releases/2010/11/101117121803.htm

[183] Judith, A. (1987). *Wheels of Life: A User's Guide to the Chakra System* (p. 327). Llewellyn Publications.

[184] Bandura, A. (1977). Self-efficacy: Toward a unifying theory of behavioral change. *Psychological Review, 84*(2), 191–215. https://doi.org/10.1037/0033-295X.84.2.191

[185] Artino, A. R. (2012). Academic Self-Efficacy: From Educational Theory to Instructional Practice. *Perspect Med Educ. 1, 76-85.* https://www.ncbi.nlm.nih.gov/pmc/articles/PMC3540350/

[186] Dweck, C. S. (2007). *Mindset: The New Psychology of Success* (pp. 7-10). Ballantine Books.

[187] Garcia, R., Bohannon, A., Farías, J., Ford, V., &Tapia, A. (2017). *The effectiveness of Efficacy programs.* Korn Ferry Institute. https://www.kornferry.com/content/dam/kornferry/docs/article-migration/EfficacyApril2017.v2.pdf

[188] Garcia, R., Bohannon, A., Farías, J., Ford, V., &Tapia, A. (2017). *The effectiveness of Efficacy programs.* Korn Ferry Institute. https://www.kornferry.com/content/dam/kornferry/docs/article-migration/EfficacyApril2017.v2.pdf

[189] Feinberg, C. (n.d.). *The Possible Dream.* Harvard Graduate School of Education. https://www.gse.harvard.edu/news/ed/04/07/possible-dream

[190] McCally, K. (2010). Self-Determined. *Rochester Review, 72*(6), 18-21. https://www.rochester.edu/pr/Review/V72N6/pdf/feature_motivation.pdf

[191] Ryan, R. M., & Deci, E. L. (2000). Self-Determination Theory and the Facilitation of Intrinsic Motivation, Social Development, and Well-Being. *American Psychologist, 55*(1), 68-78. https://selfdeterminationtheory.org/SDT/documents/2000_RyanDeci_SDT.pdf

[192] Ryan, R. M., & Deci, E. L. (2000). Self-Determination Theory and the Facilitation of Intrinsic Motivation, Social Development, and Well-Being. *American Psychologist, 55*(1), 68-78. https://selfdeterminationtheory.org/SDT/documents/2000_RyanDeci_SDT.pdf

[193] Ryan, R. M., & Deci, E. L. (2000). Self-Determination Theory and the Facilitation of Intrinsic Motivation, Social Development, and Well-Being. *American Psychologist, 55*(1), 68-78. https://selfdeterminationtheory.org/SDT/documents/2000_RyanDeci_SDT.pdf

[194] Ryan, R. M., & Deci, E. L. (2000). Self-Determination Theory and the Facilitation of Intrinsic Motivation, Social Development, and Well-Being. *American Psychologist, 55*(1), 68-78. https://selfdeterminationtheory.org/SDT/documents/2000_RyanDeci_SDT.pdf

[195] McCally, K. (2010). Self-Determined. *Rochester Review, 72*(6), 18-21. https://www.rochester.edu/pr/Review/V72N6/pdf/feature_motivation.pdf

[196] Trafton, A. (2020 October 27). *Why Motivation to Learn Declines With Age.* MIT News. https://news.mit.edu/2020/why-learn-motivate-age-decline-1027

[197] Trafton, A. (2020 October 27). *Why Motivation to Learn Declines With Age.* MIT News. https://news.mit.edu/2020/why-learn-motivate-age-decline-1027

[198] Trafton, A. (2020 October 27). *Why Motivation to Learn Declines With Age.* MIT News. https://news.mit.edu/2020/why-learn-motivate-age-decline-1027

[199] Trafton, A. (2020 October 27). *Why Motivation to Learn Declines With Age.* MIT News. https://news.mit.edu/2020/why-learn-motivate-age-decline-1027

[200] Ennis, G. E., Hess, T. M., & Smith, B. T. (2013). The impact of age and motivation on cognitive effort: implications for cognitive engagement in older adulthood. *Psychology and Aging, 28*(2), 495–504. https://doi.org/10.1037/a0031255

[201] Agarwal, P. (2018, May 17). *Free Rider Problem.* Intelligent Economist. https://www.intelligenteconomist.com/free-rider-problem/

[202] Webb, T. L., Chang, B. P. I., & Benn, Y. (2013). *'The ostrich problem': Motivated avoidance or rejection of information about goal progress.* Social and Personality Psychology Compass, 7(11), 794–807. https://doi.org/10.1111/spc3.12071

[203] Eskreis-Winkler, L. & Fishbach, A. (2020). *Hidden failures.* Organizational Behavior and Human Decision Processes, 157, 57-67. https://doi.org/10.1016/j.obhdp.2019.11.007

[204] Eskreis-Winkler, L. & Fishbach, A. (2020). *Hidden failures.* Organizational Behavior and Human Decision Processes, 157, 57-67. https://doi.org/10.1016/j.obhdp.2019.11.007

[205] Ho, T., Png, I. P. L., & Reza, S. (2017). Sunk Cost Fallacy in Driving the World's Costliest Cars. *Management Science, 64*(4), 1477-1973. https://doi.org/10.1287/mnsc.2016.2651

[206] Ho, T., Png, I. P. L., & Reza, S. (2017). Sunk Cost Fallacy in Driving the World's Costliest Cars. *Management Science, 64*(4), 1477-1973. https://doi.org/10.1287/mnsc.2016.2651

[207] Ho, T., Png, I. P. L., & Reza, S. (2017). Sunk Cost Fallacy in Driving the World's Costliest Cars. *Management Science, 64*(4), 1477-1973. https://doi.org/10.1287/mnsc.2016.2651

[208] Li, Y., Lopez-Huerta, V. G., Adiconis, X., Levandowski, K., Choi, S., Simmons, S. K., Arias-Garcia, M., Guo, B., Yao, A. Y., Blosser, T. R., Wimmer, R. D., Aida, T., Atamian, A., Naik, T., Sun, X., Bi, D., Malhotra, D., … Feng, G. (2020) Distinct subnetworks of the thalamic reticular nucleus. *Nature, 583,* 819–824. https://doi.org/10.1038/s41586-020-2504-5

[209] Kahneman, D. (2011). *Thinking, Fast and Slow.* Farrar, Strauss, and Giroux.

[210] Kahneman, D. (2011). *Thinking, Fast and Slow.* Farrar, Strauss, and Giroux.

[211] List of Cognitive Biases. (2021, July 14). In *Wikipedia.* https://en.wikipedia.org/w/index.php?title=List_of_cognitive_biases&oldid=1033568376

[212] Berger, J. G. (2019) *Unlocking Leadership Mindtraps: How to Thrive in Complexity* (p. 2). Stanford Briefs.

[213] Langewiesche, W. (2003). *Columbia's Last Flight.* The Atlantic. https://www.theatlantic.com/magazine/archive/2003/11/columbias-last-flight/304204/

[214] Howell, E. (2019, February 1). *Columbia Disaster: What happened and what NASA learned.* Space. https://www.space.com/19436-columbia-disaster.html

[215] Skitka, L. J., Hanson, B. E., Morgan, G. S., & Wisneski, D. C. (2021). The Psychology of Moral Conviction. *Annual review of psychology, 72,* 347–366. https://doi.org/10.1146/annurev-psych-063020-030612

[216] Kegan, R. & Lahey, L. L. (2009). *Immunity to Change: How to Overcome It and Unlock Potential in Yourself and Your Organization.* Harvard Business Press.

[217] Kegan, R. & Lahey, L. L. (2009). *Immunity to Change: How to Overcome It and Unlock Potential in Yourself and Your Organization.* Harvard Business Press. pp. 16-20

[218] Kegan, R. & Lahey, L. L. (2009). *Immunity to Change: How to Overcome It and Unlock Potential in Yourself and Your Organization.* Harvard Business Press. pp. 16-20

[219] Kegan, R. & Lahey, L. L. (2009). *Immunity to Change: How to Overcome It and Unlock Potential in Yourself and Your Organization.* Harvard Business Press. pp. 16-20

[220] Dahl, C. J., Lutz, A., & Davidson, R. J. (2015). Reconstructing and deconstructing the self: Cognitive mechanisms in meditation practice. *Trends in Cognitive Sciences, 19*(9), 515–523. https://doi.org/10.1016/j.tics.2015.07.001

[221] Kegan, R., & Lahey, L. L. (2009). *Immunity to Change: How to Overcome It and Unlock Potential in Yourself and Your Organization* (pp. 27-28). Harvard Business Press.

[222] Kegan, R. & Lahey, L. L. (2009). *Immunity to Change: How to Overcome It and Unlock Potential in Yourself and Your Organization.* Harvard Business Press. pp. 16-20

[223] Kegan, R., & Lahey, L. L. (2009). *Immunity to Change: How to Overcome It and Unlock Potential in Yourself and Your Organization* (pp. 27-28). Harvard Business Press.

[224] Vedantam, Shankar (Host). (2021, August 2) Cultivating Your Purpose. [Audio podcast episode]. In Hidden Brain. https://hiddenbrain.org/podcast/cultivating-your-purpose/

[225] Shultz, H. (n.d.). *Leading a Values Based Business.* Masterclass. https://www.masterclass.com/classes/howard-schultz-leading-a-values-based-business/

[226] Duckworth, A., & Gross, J. J. (2014). Self-Control and Grit: Related but Separable Determinants of Success. *Current Directions in Psychological Science, 23*(5), 319–325. https://doi.org/10.1177/0963721414541462

[227] Dave DeSteno. (n.d.) https://www.davedesteno.com

[228] DeSteno, D., Li, Y., Dickens, L., & Lerner, J. S. (2014). Gratitude: A Tool for Reducing Economic Impatience. *Psychological Science, 25*(6), 1262-1267. https://doi.org/10.1177/0956797614529979

[229] DeSteno, D., Li, Y., Dickens, L., & Lerner, J. S. (2014). Gratitude: A Tool for Reducing Economic Impatience. *Psychological Science, 25*(6), 1262-1267. https://doi.org/10.1177/0956797614529979

[230] DeSteno, D., Li, Y., Dickens, L., & Lerner, J. S. (2014). Gratitude: A Tool for Reducing Economic Impatience. *Psychological Science, 25*(6), 1262-1267. https://doi.org/10.1177/0956797614529979

[231] DeSteno, D., Li, Y., Dickens, L., & Lerner, J. S. (2014). Gratitude: A Tool for Reducing Economic Impatience. *Psychological Science, 25*(6), 1262-1267. https://doi.org/10.1177/0956797614529979

[232] Vedantam, Shankar (Host). (2021, August 2) Cultivating Your Purpose. [Audio podcast episode]. In Hidden Brain. https://hiddenbrain.org/podcast/cultivating-your-purpose/

[233] Rozin, P., & Royzman, E. B. (2001). Negativity Bias, Negativity Dominance, and Contagion. *Personality and Social Psychology Review, 5*(4), 296–320. https://doi.org/10.1207/S15327957PSPR0504_2

[234] Baumeister, R. F., Bratslavsky, E., Finkenauer, C., & Vohs, K. D. (2001). Bad is Stronger than Good. *Review of General Psychology, 5*(4), 323–370. https://doi.org/10.1037/1089-2680.5.4.323

[235] Eskreis-Winkler, L., & Fishbach, A. (2019). Not Learning from Failure—the Greatest Failure of All. *Psychological Science, 30*(12), 1733-1744. https://doi.org/10.1177/0956797619881133

[236] Eskreis-Winkler, L., & Fishbach, A. (2019). Not Learning from Failure—the Greatest Failure of All. *Psychological Science, 30*(12), 1733-1744. https://doi.org/10.1177/0956797619881133

[237] Eskreis-Winkler, L., & Fishbach, A. (2019). Not Learning from Failure—the Greatest Failure of All. *Psychological Science, 30*(12), 1733-1744. https://doi.org/10.1177/0956797619881133

[238] Colosio, M., Shestakova, A., Nikulin, V. V., Blagovechtchenski, E., & Klucharev, V. (2017). Neural Mechanisms of Cognitive Dissonance (Revised): An EEG Study. Journal of Neuroscience, 37(20), 5074-5083. https://doi.org/10.1523/JNEUROSCI.3209-16.2017

[239] Maxwell, J. C. (2000). Failing Forward: Turning Mistakes Into Stepping Stones for Success (pp. 11-22). Thomas Nelson Inc.

[240] Eknath, E. The Bhagavad Gita. Nilgiri Press, 1985.

[241] Vince, R. (1998). Behind and Beyond Kolb's Learning Cycle. *Journal of Management Education, 22*(3), 304–319. https://doi.org/10.1177/105256299802200304

[242] Vince, R. (1998). Behind and Beyond Kolb's Learning Cycle. *Journal of Management Education, 22*(3), 304–319. https://doi.org/10.1177/105256299802200304

[243] Kegan, R., & Lahey, L. (2020, May 15). *The COVID Crisis and Adult Development* [Webinar]. Harvard Graduate School of Education. https://www.gse.harvard.edu/news/uk/20/05/covid-crisis-and-adult-development

[244] Center on the Developing Child. (n.d.). *Brain Architecture*. Harvard University. https://developingchild.harvard.edu/science/key-concepts/brain-architecture/#neuron-footnote

[245] Center on the Developing Child. (n.d.). *Brain Architecture*. Harvard University. https://developingchild.harvard.edu/science/key-concepts/brain-architecture/#neuron-footnote

[246] Center on the Developing Child. (n.d.). *Brain Architecture*. Harvard University. https://developingchild.harvard.edu/science/key-concepts/brain-architecture/#neuron-footnote

[247] Center on the Developing Child. (n.d.). *Brain Architecture*. Harvard University. https://developingchild.harvard.edu/science/key-concepts/brain-architecture/#neuron-footnote

[248] Kornfield, Jack. *The Beauty of Beginner's Mind.* https://jackkornfield.com/beginners-mind/

[249] Kahneman, D. (2013). *Thinking, Fast and Slow* (p. 13). Farrar, Straus and Giroux.

[250] Center on the Developing Child. (n.d.). *Brain Architecture*. Harvard University. https://developingchild.harvard.edu/science/key-concepts/brain-architecture/#neuron-footnote

[251] Gilbert, D. (2014). *The Psychology of Your Future Self* [Video]. TED. https://www.ted.com/talks/dan_gilbert_the_psychology_of_your_future_self?language=en

[252] Schippers, M. C., & Ziegler, N. (2019). Life Crafting as a Way to Find Purpose and Meaning in Life. *Frontiers in Psychology, 10.* https://doi.org/10.3389/fpsyg.2019.02778

[253] Schippers, M. C., & Ziegler, N. (2019). Life Crafting as a Way to Find Purpose and Meaning in Life. *Frontiers in Psychology, 10.* https://doi.org/10.3389/fpsyg.2019.02778

[254] Johnson, Whitney (Host). (2020, November 17). James Clear: Atomic Habits. (No. 190) [Audio podcast episode]. In *Disrupt Yourself.* https://whitneyjohnson.com/james-clear-encore/

[255] Levitt, S., & Dubner, S. J. (2010). *Freakonomics: A Rogue Economist Explores the Hidden Side of Everything* (Revised, Expanded ed.). William Morrow.

[256] Schelling, T. (1956). An Essay on Bargaining. *The American Economic Review, 46*(3), 281-306. http://www.jstor.org/stable/1805498

[257] Clear, J. (2018). *Atomic Habits: An Easy & Proven Way to Build Good Habits & Break Bad Ones.* Avery.

[258] Clear, J. (2018). *Atomic Habits: An Easy & Proven Way to Build Good Habits & Break Bad Ones.* Avery.

[259] Johnson, Whitney (Host). (2020, November 17). James Clear: Atomic Habits. (No. 190) [Audio podcast episode]. In *Disrupt Yourself.* https://whitneyjohnson.com/james-clear-encore/

[260] Stanchfield, J. (2013, December 18). *The Brain, Learning, and Reflection.* Experiential Tools. https://blog.experientialtools.com/2013/12/18/the-brain-learning-and-reflection/

[261] Morning Edition. (2007, March 8). *'Embrace the Suck' and More Military Speak* [Radio Broadcast]. NPR. https://www.npr.org/2007/03/08/7458809/embrace-the-suck-and-more-military-speak

[262] Vygotsky, L. S. (1978). *Mind in Society: The Development of Higher Psychological Processes.* Harvard University Press. https://doi.org/10.2307/j.ctvjf9vz4

[263] Bandura, A. (1977). Self-efficacy: Toward a unifying theory of behavioral change. *Psychological Review, 84*(2), 191–215. https://doi.org/10.1037/0033-295X.84.2.191

[264] Yankner, B. A., Lu, T., & Loerch, P. (2008). The Aging Brain. *Annual Review of Pathology: Mechanisms of Disease, 3,* 41-66. https://doi.org/10.1146/annurev.pathmechdis.2.010506.092044

[265] Pannese, E. (2011). Morphological changes in nerve cells during normal aging. *Brain Structure and Function. 216,* 85–89. https://doi.org/10.1007/s00429-011-0308-y

[266] Pannese, E. (2011). Morphological changes in nerve cells during normal aging. *Brain Structure and Function. 216*, 85–89. https://doi.org/10.1007/s00429-011-0308-y

[267] Shimada, A., & Hasegawa-Ishii, S. (2011). Senescence-accelerated Mice (SAMs) as a Model for Brain Aging and Immunosenescence. *Aging and disease, 2*(5), 414–435.

[268] Pannese, E. (2011). Morphological changes in nerve cells during normal aging. *Brain Structure and Function. 216*, 85–89. https://doi.org/10.1007/s00429-011-0308-y

[269] Goh, . O. & Park, D. C. (2009). Neuroplasticity and cognitive aging: The scaffolding theory of aging and cognition. *Restorative Neurology and Neuroscience, 27*(5), 391-403. https://content.iospress.com/articles/restorative-neurology-and-neuroscience/rnn00493

[270] Berthold, E. (2018, April 10). *What Are Telomeres?* Australian Academy of Science. https://www.science.org.au/curious/people-medicine/what-are-telomeres

[271] Shammas, M. A. (2011). Telomeres, lifestyle, cancer, and aging. *Current Opinion in Clinical Nutrition and Metabolic Care, 14*(1), 28–34. https://doi.org/10.1097/MCO.0b013e32834121b1

[272] Max Planck Institute for Human Cognitive and Brain Sciences. (2019, September 27). *Cellular aging is linked to structural changes in the brain: Telomeres on human chromosomes change together with brain structure.* ScienceDaily. www.sciencedaily.com/releases/2019/09/190927103248.htm

[273] Shammas, M. A. (2011). Telomeres, lifestyle, cancer, and aging. *Current Opinion in Clinical Nutrition and Metabolic Care, 14*(1), 28–34. https://doi.org/10.1097/MCO.0b013e32834121b1

[274] Max Planck Institute for Human Cognitive and Brain Sciences. (2019, September 27). *Cellular aging is linked to structural changes in the brain: Telomeres on human chromosomes change together with brain structure.* ScienceDaily. www.sciencedaily.com/releases/2019/09/190927103248.htm

[275] Fuchs, E., & Flügge, G. (2014). Adult Neuroplasticity: More Than 40 Years of Research. *Neural Plasticity, 2014.* https://doi.org/10.1155/2014/541870

[276] McEwen, B. S., Nasca, C., & Gray, J. D. (2016). Stress Effects on Neuronal Structure: Hippocampus, Amygdala, and Prefrontal Cortex. *Neuropsychopharmacology, 41*, 3–23. https://doi.org/10.1038/npp.2015.171

[277] Fuchs, E., & Flügge, G. (2014). Adult Neuroplasticity: More Than 40 Years of Research. *Neural Plasticity, 2014.* https://doi.org/10.1155/2014/541870

[278] Kim, E. J., Pellman, B., & Kim, J. J. (2015). Stress effects on the hippocampus: a critical review. *Learning & memory (Cold Spring Harbor), 22*(9), 411–416. https://doi.org/10.1101/lm.037291.114

[279] van der Kolk, B. (2014). *The Body Keeps the Score: Brain, Mind, Body in the Healing of Trauma.* Viking.

[280] van der Kolk, B. (2014). *The Body Keeps the Score: Brain, Mind, Body in the Healing of Trauma.* Viking.

[281] Ornish, D. (2008, March). *Your Genes Are Not Your Fate* [Video]. TED. https://www.ted.com/talks/dean_ornish_your_genes_are_not_your_fate

[282] Dougherty, R. J., Schultz, S. A., Kirby, T. K., Boots, E. A., Oh, J. M., Edwards, D., Gallagher, C. L., Carlsson, C. M., Bendlin, B. B., Asthana, S., Sager, M. A., Hermann, B. P., Christian, B. T., Johnson, S. C., Cook, D. B., & Okonkwo, O. C. (2017). Moderate Physical Activity is Associated with Cerebral Glucose Metabolism in Adults at Risk for Alzheimer's Disease. *Journal of Alzheimer's disease : JAD, 58*(4), 1089–1097. https://doi.org/10.3233/JAD-161067

[283] Snigdha, S., de Rivera, C., Milgram, N. W., & Cotman, C. W. (2014). Exercise enhances memory consolidation in the aging brain. *Frontiers in aging neuroscience, 6*, 3. https://doi.org/10.3389/fnagi.2014.00003

[284] Urcelay, G. P., & Miller, R. R. (2008). Retrieval from Memory. *Learning and Memory: A Comprehensive Reference, 1,* 53-73. https://doi.org/10.1016/B978-012370509-9.00075-9

[285] Snigdha, S., de Rivera, C., Milgram, N. W., & Cotman, C. W. (2014). Exercise enhances memory consolidation in the aging brain. *Frontiers in aging neuroscience, 6*, 3. https://doi.org/10.3389/fnagi.2014.00003

[286] Cole, G. M., Ma, Q. L., & Frautschy, S. A. (2010). Dietary fatty acids and the aging brain. *Nutrition Reviews, 68*(Suppl. 2), S102–S111. https://doi.org/10.1111/j.1753-4887.2010.00345.x

[287] Su, H. (2010). Mechanisms of n-3 fatty acid-mediated development and maintenance of learning memory performance. *The Journal of Nutritional Biochemistry, 21*(5), 364–373. https://doi.org/10.1016/j.jnutbio.2009.11.003

[288] Abbott, K. N., Arnott, C. K., Westbrook, R. F., & Tran, D. (2019). The effect of high fat, high sugar, and combined high fat-high sugar diets on spatial learning and memory in rodents: A meta-analysis. *Neuroscience & Biobehavioral Reviews, 107*, 399-421. https://doi.org/10.1016/j.neubiorev.2019.08.010

[289] Molteni, R., Barnard, R. J., Ying, Z., Roberts, C. K., & Gómez-Pinilla, F. (2002). A high-fat, refined sugar diet reduces hippocampal brain-derived neurotrophic factor, neuronal plasticity, and learning. *Neuroscience, 112*(4), 803-814. https://doi.org/10.1016/S0306-4522(02)00123-9

[290] Molteni, R., Barnard, R. J., Ying, Z., Roberts, C. K., & Gómez-Pinilla, F. (2002). A high-fat, refined sugar diet reduces hippocampal brain-derived neurotrophic factor, neuronal plasticity, and learning. *Neuroscience, 112*(4), 803-814. https://doi.org/10.1016/S0306-4522(02)00123-9

[291] Goleman, D., & Davidson, R. J. (2017). *Altered Traits: Science Reveals How Meditation Changes Your Mind, Brain, and Body.* Avery.

[292] MBSR was founded by Jon Kabat-Zinn. Goleman, D., & Davidson, R. J. (2017). *Altered Traits: Science Reveals How Meditation Changes Your Mind, Brain, and Body*. Avery. p. 3

[293] Goleman, D., & Davidson, R. J. (2017). *Altered Traits: Science Reveals How Meditation Changes Your Mind, Brain, and Body*. Avery. p. 98.

[294] Goleman, D., & Davidson, R. J. (2017). *Altered Traits: Science Reveals How Meditation Changes Your Mind, Brain, and Body*. Avery. p. 251.

[295] Goleman, D., & Davidson, R. J. (2017). *Altered Traits: Science Reveals How Meditation Changes Your Mind, Brain, and Body*. Avery. 180

[296] Goleman, D., & Davidson, R. J. (2017). *Altered Traits: Science Reveals How Meditation Changes Your Mind, Brain, and Body*. Avery. p. 176.

[297] Iyengar, B. K. S. (1979). *Light on Yoga: The Bible of Modern Yoga* (p. 19). Schocken.

[298] Iyengar, B. K. S. (1979). *Light on Yoga: The Bible of Modern Yoga* (p. 19). Schocken.

[299] The International Association of Yoga Therapists. (n.d.). *Contemporary Definitions of Yoga Therapy*. https://www.iayt.org/page/ContemporaryDefiniti

[300] Sullivan, M. B., Erb, M., Schmalzl, L., Moonaz, S., Noggle Taylor, J., & Porges, S. W. (2018). Yoga Therapy and Polyvagal Theory: The Convergence of Traditional Wisdom and Contemporary Neuroscience for Self-Regulation and Resilience. *Frontiers in Human Neuroscience, 12*. https://doi.org/10.3389/fnhum.2018.00067

[301] Sullivan, M. B., Erb, M., Schmalzl, L., Moonaz, S., Noggle Taylor, J., & Porges, S. W. (2018). Yoga Therapy and Polyvagal Theory: The Convergence of Traditional Wisdom and Contemporary Neuroscience for Self-Regulation and Resilience. *Frontiers in Human Neuroscience, 12*. https://doi.org/10.3389/fnhum.2018.00067

[302] Sullivan, M. B., Erb, M., Schmalzl, L., Moonaz, S., Noggle Taylor, J., & Porges, S. W. (2018). Yoga Therapy and Polyvagal Theory: The Convergence of Traditional Wisdom and Contemporary Neuroscience for Self-Regulation and Resilience. *Frontiers in Human Neuroscience, 12*. https://doi.org/10.3389/fnhum.2018.00067

[303] van der Kolk, B. (2014). *The Body Keeps the Score: Brain, Mind, Body in the Healing of Trauma*. Viking.

[304] Rasch, B., & Born, J. (2013). About Sleep's Role in Memory. *Physiological Reviews, 93*(2), 681–766. https://doi.org/10.1152/physrev.00032.2012

[305] McClelland, J. L., & Goddard, N. H. (1996). Considerations arising from a complementary learning systems perspective on hippocampus and neocortex. *Hippocampus, 6*(6), 654-665. https://doi.org/10.1002/(SICI)1098-1063(1996)6:6<654::AID-HIPO8>3.0.CO;2-G

[306] McClelland, J. L., & Goddard, N. H. (1996). Considerations arising from a complementary learning systems perspective on hippocampus and neocortex.

Hippocampus, 6(6), 654-665. https://doi.org/10.1002/(SICI)1098-1063(1996)6:6<654::AID-HIPO8>3.0.CO;2-G

[307] Rasch, B., & Born, J. (2013). About Sleep's Role in Memory. *Physiological Reviews, 93*(2), 681–766. https://doi.org/10.1152/physrev.00032.2012

[308] Ruch, S., & Henke, K. (2020). Learning During Sleep: A Dream Comes True? *Trends in Cognitive Science, 24*(3), 170-172. https://doi.org/10.1016/j.tics.2019.12.007

[309] Ruch, S., & Henke, K. (2020). Learning During Sleep: A Dream Comes True? *Trends in Cognitive Science, 24*(3), 170-172. https://doi.org/10.1016/j.tics.2019.12.007

[310] Lee, M., Lee, Y., Hwang, Y. H., Min, A., Han, B. S., & Kim, D. Y. (2016). Impact of sleep restriction on the structural brain network. NeuroReport, 27(18), 1299-1304. https://doi.org/10.1097/WNR.0000000000000687

[311] Jessen, N. A., Munk, A. S., Lundgaard, I., & Nedergaard, M. (2015). The Glymphatic System: A Beginner's Guide. *Neurochemical research, 40*(12), 2583–2599. https://doi.org/10.1007/s11064-015-1581-6

[312] Jessen, N. A., Munk, A. S., Lundgaard, I., & Nedergaard, M. (2015). The Glymphatic System: A Beginner's Guide. *Neurochemical research, 40*(12), 2583–2599. https://doi.org/10.1007/s11064-015-1581-6

[313] Xie, L., Kang, H., Xu, Q., Chen, M. J., Liao, Y., Thiyagarajan, M., O'Donnell, J., Christensen, D. J., Nicholson, C., Iliff, J. J., Takano, T., Deane, R., & Nedergaard, M. (2013). Sleep drives metabolite clearance from the adult brain. *Science, 342*(6156), 373–377. https://doi.org/10.1126/science.1241224

[314] Xie, L., Kang, H., Xu, Q., Chen, M. J., Liao, Y., Thiyagarajan, M., O'Donnell, J., Christensen, D. J., Nicholson, C., Iliff, J. J., Takano, T., Deane, R., & Nedergaard, M. (2013). Sleep drives metabolite clearance from the adult brain. *Science, 342*(6156), 373–377. https://doi.org/10.1126/science.1241224

[315] Bjork, E., & Bjork, R. A. (2011) Making things hard on yourself, but in a good way: Creating desirable difficulties to enhance learning. *Psychology and the real world, 2.* https://www.researchgate.net/publication/284097727_Making_things_hard_on_yourself_but_in_a_good_way_Creating_desirable_difficulties_to_enhance_learning

[316] Bjork, E., & Bjork, R. A. (2011) Making things hard on yourself, but in a good way: Creating desirable difficulties to enhance learning. *Psychology and the real world, 2.* https://www.researchgate.net/publication/284097727_Making_things_hard_on_yourself_but_in_a_good_way_Creating_desirable_difficulties_to_enhance_learning

[317] Bjork, E., & Bjork, R. A. (2011) Making things hard on yourself, but in a good way: Creating desirable difficulties to enhance learning. *Psychology and the real world, 2.* https://www.researchgate.net/publication/284097727_Making_things_hard_o

n_yourself_but_in_a_good_way_Creating_desirable_difficulties_to_enhance_learning.

[318] Karpicke, J. D. (2017). Retrieval-Based Learning: A Decade of Progress. *Learning and Memory: A Comprehensive Reference* (Second Edition), 487-514. http://dx.doi.org/10.1016/B978-0-12-809324-5.21055-9

[319] Bjork, E., & Bjork, R. A. (2011) Making things hard on yourself, but in a good way: Creating desirable difficulties to enhance learning. *Psychology and the real world, 2.*
https://www.researchgate.net/publication/284097727_Making_things_hard_on_yourself_but_in_a_good_way_Creating_desirable_difficulties_to_enhance_learning

[320] Bjork, E., & Bjork, R. A. (2011) Making things hard on yourself, but in a good way: Creating desirable difficulties to enhance learning. *Psychology and the real world, 2.*
https://www.researchgate.net/publication/284097727_Making_things_hard_on_yourself_but_in_a_good_way_Creating_desirable_difficulties_to_enhance_learning

[321] Bjork, E., & Bjork, R. A. (2011) Making things hard on yourself, but in a good way: Creating desirable difficulties to enhance learning. *Psychology and the real world, 2.*
https://www.researchgate.net/publication/284097727_Making_things_hard_on_yourself_but_in_a_good_way_Creating_desirable_difficulties_to_enhance_learning

[322] Walsh, M. M., Gluck, K. A., Gunzelmann, G., Jastrzembski, T., Krusmark, M., Myung, J. I., Pitt, M. A., & Zhou, R. (2018). Mechanisms underlying the spacing effect in learning: A comparison of three computational models. *Journal of Experimental Psychology: General, 147*(9), 1325–1348. https://doi.org/10.1037/xge0000416

[323] Roosevelt, E. (2009). *You Learn by Living: Eleven keys for a More Fulfilling Life.* Westminster John Knox Press.

[324] Zhang, S., Verguts, T., Zhang, C., Feng, P., Chen, Q., & Feng, T. (2021). Outcome Value and Task Aversiveness Impact Task Procrastination through Separate Neural Pathways. Cerebral Cortex, 31(8), 3846-3855. https://doi.org/10.1093/cercor/bhab053

[325] Zhang, S., Verguts, T., Zhang, C., Feng, P., Chen, Q., & Feng, T. (2021). Outcome Value and Task Aversiveness Impact Task Procrastination through Separate Neural Pathways. Cerebral Cortex, 31(8), 3846-3855. https://doi.org/10.1093/cercor/bhab053

[326] Chen, Z., Liu, P., Zhang, C., & Feng, T. (2020). Brain Morphological Dynamics of Procrastination: The Crucial Role of the Self-Control, Emotional, and Episodic Prospection Network. *Cerebral Cortex, 30*(5), 2834–2853. https://doi.org/10.1093/cercor/bhz278

[327] Lyons, I. M., & Beilock, S. L. (2012). When Math Hurts: Math Anxiety Predicts Pain Network Activation in Anticipation of Doing Math. *PLOS ONE, 7*(10). https://doi.org/10.1371/journal.pone.0048076

[328] van Eerde, W., & Klingsieck, K. B. (2018). Overcoming procrastination? A meta-analysis of intervention studies. *Educational Research Review, 25,* 73-85. https://doi.org/10.1016/j.edurev.2018.09.002

[329] van Eerde, W., & Klingsieck, K. B. (2018). Overcoming procrastination? A meta-analysis of intervention studies. *Educational Research Review, 25,* 73-85. https://doi.org/10.1016/j.edurev.2018.09.002

[330] Bubbico, G., Chiacchiaretta, P., Parenti, M., di Marco, M., Panara, V., Sepede, G., Ferretti, A., & Perrucci, G. (2019). Effects of Second Language Learning on the Plastic Aging Brain: Functional Connectivity, Cognitive Decline and Reorganization. *Frontiers in Neuroscience, 13.* https://doi.org/10.3389/fnins.2019.00423

[331] Nestojko, J. F., Bui, D. C., Kornell, N., & Bjork, E. L. (2014). Expecting to teach enhances learning and organization of knowledge in free recall of text passages. *Memory & cognition, 42*(7), 1038–1048. https://doi.org/10.3758/s13421-014-0416-z

[332] Daou, M., Lohse, K. R., & Miller, M. W. (2016). Expecting to teach enhances motor learning and information processing during practice. *Human movement science, 49,* 336–345. https://doi.org/10.1016/j.humov.2016.08.009

[333] Daou, M., Lohse, K. R., & Miller, M. W. (2016). Expecting to teach enhances motor learning and information processing during practice. *Human movement science, 49,* 336–345. https://doi.org/10.1016/j.humov.2016.08.009

[334] TEDx Talks. (2014, August 5.) *Learning how to learn | Barbara Oakley | TEDxOaklandUniversity* [Video]. Youtube. https://www.youtube.com/watch?v=O96fE1E-rf8&t=332s

[335] TEDx Talks. (2014, August 5.) *Learning how to learn | Barbara Oakley | TEDxOaklandUniversity* [Video]. Youtube. https://www.youtube.com/watch?v=O96fE1E-rf8&t=332s

[336] Marron, T. R., Berant, E., Axelrod, V., & Faust, M. (2020). Spontaneous cognition and its relationship to human creativity: A functional connectivity study involving a chain free association task. *NeuroImage, 220,* Article 117064. https://doi.org/10.1016/j.neuroimage.2020.117064

[337] TEDx Talks. (2014, August 5.) *Learning how to learn | Barbara Oakley | TEDxOaklandUniversity* [Video]. Youtube. https://www.youtube.com/watch?v=O96fE1E-rf8&t=332s

[338] Marron, T. R., Berant, E., Axelrod, V., & Faust, M. (2020). Spontaneous cognition and its relationship to human creativity: A functional connectivity study involving a chain free association task. *NeuroImage, 220,* Article 117064. https://doi.org/10.1016/j.neuroimage.2020.117064

[339] Andrews-Hanna J. R. (2012). The brain's default network and its adaptive role in internal mentation. *The Neuroscientist : a review journal bringing*

neurobiology, neurology and psychiatry, 18(3), 251–270. https://doi.org/10.1177/1073858411403316

340 TEDx Talks. (2014, August 5.) *Learning how to learn | Barbara Oakley | TEDxOaklandUniversity* [Video]. Youtube. https://www.youtube.com/watch?v=O96fE1E-rf8&t=332s

341 Christoff, K., Gordon, A., & Smith, R. (2011). The role of spontaneous thought in human cognition. In O. Vartanian & D. R. Mandel (Eds.), *Neuroscience of decision making* (pp. 259–284). Psychology Press.

342 Jenkins, J. G., & Dallenbach, K. M. (1924). Obliviscence during sleep and waking. *The American Journal of Psychology, 35*(4), 605-612. https://doi.org/10.2307/1414040

343 Sara, S. J. (2017). Sleep to Remember. *Journal of Neuroscience, 37*(3), 457-463. https://doi.org/10.1523/JNEUROSCI.0297-16.2017

344 Sara, S. J. (2017). Sleep to Remember. *Journal of Neuroscience, 37*(3), 457-463. https://doi.org/10.1523/JNEUROSCI.0297-16.2017

345 Sara, S. J. (2017). Sleep to Remember. *Journal of Neuroscience, 37*(3), 457-463. https://doi.org/10.1523/JNEUROSCI.0297-16.2017

346 Cann, O. (2018, September 17). *Machines Will Do More Tasks Than Humans by 2025 but Robot Revolution Will Still Create 58 Million Net New Jobs in Next Five Years.* World Economic Forum. https://www.weforum.org/press/2018/09/machines-will-do-more-tasks-than-humans-by-2025-but-robot-revolution-will-still-create-58-million-net-new-jobs-in-next-five-years/

347 Kearney. (n.d.). *The state of human factory analytics.* https://www.kearney.com/digital/the-state-of-human-factory-analytics

348 Zahidi, S., Ratcheva, V., Hingel, G., & Brown, S. (2020, October). *The Future of Jobs Report.* World Economic Forum. http://www3.weforum.org/docs/WEF_Future_of_Jobs_2020.pdf

349 Zahidi, S., Ratcheva, V., Hingel, G., & Brown, S. (2020, October). *The Future of Jobs Report.* World Economic Forum. http://www3.weforum.org/docs/WEF_Future_of_Jobs_2020.pdf

350 Kegan, R., & Lahey, L. L. (2009). *Immunity to Change: How to Overcome It and Unlock Potential in Yourself and Your Organization* (p. 6). Harvard Business Press.

351 Von Ahn, L., Blum, M., Hopper, N. J., & Langford, J. (2003). CAPTCHA: Using Hard AI Problems for Security. *Advances in Cryptology — EUROCRYPT 2003*, 294–311. https://doi.org/10.1007/3-540-39200-9_18

352 Turing, A. M. (950). Computing Machinery and Intelligence. *Mind, 59*(236), 433-460. https://doi.org/10.1093/mind/LIX.236.433

353 Guerar, M., Verderame, L., Migliardi, M., Palmieri, F., & Merlo, A. (2021). *Gotta CAPTCHA 'Em All: A Survey of Twenty years of the Human-or-Computer Dilemma.* https://arxiv.org/abs/2103.01748

354 Google. (n.d.). *Recaptcha.* https://www.google.com/recaptcha/about/

[355] Shet, V. (2014, December 3). Are you a robot? Introducing "No CAPTCHA reCAPTCHA". *Google Security Blog.* https://security.googleblog.com/2014/12/are-you-robot-introducing-no-captcha.html

[356] Shet, V. (2014, December 3). Are you a robot? Introducing "No CAPTCHA reCAPTCHA". *Google Security Blog.* https://security.googleblog.com/2014/12/are-you-robot-introducing-no-captcha.html

[357] Shet, V. (2014, December 3). Are you a robot? Introducing "No CAPTCHA reCAPTCHA". *Google Security Blog.* https://security.googleblog.com/2014/12/are-you-robot-introducing-no-captcha.html

[358] IBM. (n.d.). *Artificial Intelligence.* https://www.ibm.com/security/artificial-intelligence

[359] IBM. (n.d.). *Artificial Intelligence.* https://www.ibm.com/security/artificial-intelligence

[360] https://www.history.com/topics/great-depression/dust-bowl

[361] Worldometer. (2021, September 7). *Coronavirus Death Toll.* https://www.worldometers.info/coronavirus/coronavirus-death-toll/

[362] The National Intelligence Council. (2021, March). *The COVID-19 Factor: Expanding Uncertainty.* Global Trends. https://www.dni.gov/index.php/gt2040-home/summary/the-covid-factor

[363] Mark, J. J. (2020, April 16). *Effects of the Black Death on Europe.* World History Encyclopedia. https://www.ancient.eu/article/1543/effects-of-the-black-death-on-europe/

[364] Mark, J. J. (2020, April 16). *Effects of the Black Death on Europe.* World History Encyclopedia. https://www.ancient.eu/article/1543/effects-of-the-black-death-on-europe/

[365] Burckhardt, J., Murray, P. (Ed.). (1990). *The Civilization of the Renaissance in Italy,* pp. 9-12 (S. G. C. Middlemore, Trans.). Penguin Classics. (Original work published 1860)

[366] Centers for Disease Control and Prevention. (2018, March 21). *History of 1918 Flu Pandemic.* https://www.cdc.gov/flu/pandemic-resources/1918-commemoration/1918-pandemic-history.htm

[367] Worldometer. (2021, September 7). *Coronavirus Death Toll.* https://www.worldometers.info/coronavirus/coronavirus-death-toll/

[368] Worldometer. (n.d.). *World Population by Year.* https://www.worldometers.info/world-population/world-population-by-year/

[369] Worldometer. (n.d.). *World Population Projections.* https://www.worldometers.info/world-population/world-population-projections/

[370] Maas, S. (2020, May). *Social and Economic Impacts of the 1918 Influenza Pandemic.* National Bureau of Economic Research.

https://www.nber.org/digest/may20/social-and-economic-impacts-1918-influenza-epidemic

[371] Roos, D. (2020, April 28,). *When WWI, Pandemic and Slump Ended, Americans Sprung Into the Roaring Twenties.* History. https://www.history.com/news/pandemic-world-war-i-roaring-twenties

[372] Maas, S. (2020, May). *Social and Economic Impacts of the 1918 Influenza Pandemic.* National Bureau of Economic Research. https://www.nber.org/digest/may20/social-and-economic-impacts-1918-influenza-epidemic

[373] Spinney, L. (2017, September 27). *How the 1918 Flu Pandemic Revolutionized Public Health.* Smithsonian Magazine. https://www.smithsonianmag.com/history/how-1918-flu-pandemic-revolutionized-public-health-180965025/

[374] Billing, F., De Smet, A., Reich, A., Schaninger, B., & Seiler, D (Ed.). (2021, April 30). *Building workforce skills at scale to thrive during – and after – the COVID-19 crisis.* McKinsey & Company. https://www.mckinsey.com/business-functions/organization/our-insights/building-workforce-skills-at-scale-to-thrive-during-and-after-the-covid-19-crisis

[375] Harris, S. (Host). (2021, August 13). The State of the World: A Conversation with Dambisa Moyo (No. 257) [Audio Podcast Episode]. In *Making Sense.* Sam Harris. https://samharris.org/podcasts/257-state-world/

[376] Carse, J. P. (2013). *Finite and Infinite Games: A vision of life as play and possibility* (p. 62). Free Press.